Robert Klanten / Lukas Feireiss (Eds.)

[STRIKE A POSE].

ECCENTRIC ARCHITECTURE AND SPECTACULAR SPACES.

gestalten

[STRIKE A POSE].

CONTENT/

ECCENTRIC ARCHITECTURE AND SPECTACULAR SPACES.

CONTRIBUTORS:

3deluxe, 3 Gatti, 5+1AA, A.H.Architects, Ab Rogers Design, Adamo-Faiden, Akihito Fumita Design Office, Akiyoshi Takagi, Alphaville, Alvaro Siza, Amorphe, Andy Tong Creations, Aoki Jun, Architecture Lab, Architectural Body Research Foundation, Arquitectonica, Asymptote, Atelier Bow-Wow, Atelier Hitoshi Abe, Atelier Tekuto, Barkow Leibinger, Baupiloten, Behet Bondzio Lin, Bernard Khoury / DW5, Biehler Weith Associated, BIG Bjarke Ingels Group, BINC Interiorstuff, Black Kosloff Knott Pty Ltd , Böge Lindner Architekten, Brisac-Gonzalez, Cadaval & Solà-Morales, Chris Bosse, Cloud 9, Coast Office, Coop Himmelb(l)au, Curiosity Jp, Studio Daniel Libeskind, DSDHA, E2MN, Eduardo Longo, Electric Dreams, Embaixada Arquitectura, Enric Miralles Benedetta Tagliabue, FAK3, Fashion Architecture Taste , Franklin Azzi, Frohn & Rojas / FAR, Gerd Couckhuyt, Giorgio Borruso Design, Graft, Hertl Architekten, Herzog & De Meuron, Hirofumi Ohno, Hiroshi Nakamura & NAP Co., Hudson Architects, Isay Weinfeld, ISSHO Architects, J. Mayer H. Architects, Jarmund/Vigsnæs, Metro Arquitetura, Karim Rashid, Katsuhiro Miyamoto & Associates, Kazuyo Seijima + Ryue Nishizawa / SANAA, Kiyonobu Nakagame Architect and Associates, Klein Dytham Architecture, Kochi Architect's Studio, Küger Schuberth Vandreike, KWK Promes, Lab Architecture, LAR / Fernando Romero, Lot-Ek, Lyons, MAD Office, Make Architects, Manuelle Gautrand, Masahiro Ikeda, Mass Studies, Meixner Schlüter Wendt Architekten, Menis Arquitectos, MOS, MVRDV, N Maeda Atelier, nArchitects, NAYA Architects, Neil M. Denari Architects, Netzwerk Architekten, Neutelings Riedijk Architecten, Nikken Sekkei, NKS Architects, No.mad Arquitectos, NRAP / Nicholas Ray and Plastik Architects, Office for Metropolitan Architecture, Ofis Arhitekti, Paul Andreu, Paul Morgan Architects, Périphériques Architectes, Peter Grundmann, Peter Kulka, Pott Architects, Powerhouse Company, Preston Scott Cohen, Procter Rihl, Queeste Architecten, Robert Neun, Rojkind Arquitectos, Schemata Architecture, sciSKEW Collaborative, Serero Architects, Serie London, Shogo Aratani Architect & Associates, Staat Amsterdam, Stan Allen Architects, Studio 63,, Studio Arne Quinze , Studio M, Tatiana Bilbao, Teradadesign Architects, Tezuka Architects, Tham & Videgard Hanson Arkitekter, Thom Faulders, Tommie Wilhelmsen, Tony Owen NDM Architects, UN Studio, Villa Eugénie, Wandel Hoefer Lorch Architekten, Wolfgang Tschapeller, Wonderwall Inc., Yuji Nakae, Yukio Asari, Zaha Hadid Architects, Zanderroth Architekten.

PREFACE:

There is something extremely addictive about architecture. Once it gets hold of you, it's almost impossible to let go. This is partly due to architecture's ubiquitous and universal nature. Our entire life is literally embedded in architecture. We are constantly surrounded, affected and shaped by it – whether consciously perceived or unconsciously experienced.

It is therefore of no surprise that multiple creative alliances are forged with other disciplines. Yet the only other discipline that seems to be able to compete with architecture's exceptional omnipresence in its individual experience is probably music. Just like architecture, music enwraps and encloses its audience. On a par with one another, they both succeed in creating highly pervasive environments. Even though they exist independently and irrespectively of each other, ideas from both of these two spheres of creativity interact and penetrate from one area into another, being mutually complementary. The apparent overlap between form and space in audible and visible terms emphatically comes to the fore in Goethe's already classic characterization of architecture as frozen music. Taking this famous quote as a playful starting point for the overall composition and conception of the book, STRIKE A POSE alludes to the interplay between music and architecture in its nominal reference to excerpts from songs of popular music.

By establishing this metaphorical relationship between the realm of pop music and the examples of contemporary architecture projects presented in this book, new areas of imaginative response are cultivated that allow us to associate the one with the other – without thereby raising any claim of integrity in this undertaking. It is therfore by no means my intention to raise a serious discussion on the matter here, but to freely adopt and employ attributes and slogans from the world of popular culture to enhance the accessibility of contemporary building practices well beyond disciplinary boundaries. A striking posture and attitude is deliberately and excessively assumed for this purpose, conveying the dramatic power of gesture, pose and image within architecture. The architecture itself becomes the show to which the spectator comes not only to see the play, but also to feel a new attitude towards space and new understanding of the world. To speak of architecture is to articulate who we are, how we want to live, and what our society does or should look like.

Against this backdrop, STRIKE A POSE warmly welcomes the future with its forward-thinking examples, ranging from interior design to homes and large-scale buildings. In doing so the kaleidoscopic spectrum of work featured in this book very well demonstrates today's perspectives and possibilities in these fields of activity. The work is current and international in scope, and examples are drawn from a wide range of practice. With regard to their formalistic language, some of the them speak gently but assertively in contained self-confidence; others convey their message in seemingly frenetic outbursts and free-flowing creative impulses; others again express themselves in humorous interrogations and re-creations of traditional concepts and values. Despite the broad range of origins, aims and outcomes, the projects are assembled in four exemplary chapters that respectively highlight one of their key features but remain essentially open for reciprocal exchange.

The first chapter, TRAMP, inspired by Otis Redding's 1967 hit single of the same title, looks at eccentric stand-alone architectures situated away from the bustle of urban life that defy conventions of traditional building practices and draw their inspiration from nature and their environments.

The projects in the ABSTRACT PLANE chapter, influenced by Frank Black's song of the same name, move within the urban context and vividly illustrate the creative richness that emerges when thinking out of the box. The examples here range from private residences to public buildings, opera houses and museums – to mention only a few. In their formal vocabulary they move from minimalistic to ever more complex styles that appropriately convey an impression of the diverse language of architectural forms today.

TRUE COLORS is about architectural feasts for the eye that don't shy away from ardently committing themselves to the full spectrum of colours. The projects presented in this chapter, inspired by Cyndi Lauper's second album of the same name from 1986, include amongst others a number of impressive interiors, daring event designs, renovations of existing building structures from the inside out, light installations and entire blocks of buildings.

The concluding chapter CRAZY DIAMOND pays a tribute by name to Pink Floyd's 1976 title "Shine On You Crazy Diamond", and traces a wide variety of projects that seem to seek inspiration from crystalline forms and lucid structures. Here, projects are aligned that encompass everything from small-scale interior designs to high-rise buildings for which only the sky seems to be the limit.

All in all, STRIKE A POSE tries to give architecture back the fun that it often misses and takes the reader on a passionate cruise around the world, to witness the emergence of profoundly new types of architectures. An inborn desire to experiment, to dispute the accepted and to enjoy the delights of form and space is palpable in all of the projects. In a kind of radical euphoria they explore the hedonistic possibilities of architecture in a playground of tantalizing forms, spectacular structures and sublime superficialities. The projects at hand exhibit a relish for the extreme and the outrageous. They break original and new ground in the field of architecture and beyond, not only in their futuristic design but also in their chromatic intensity and charged iconicity.

The approach is indeed over-simplified but nothing more was ever intended. So enjoy the surface, and, in the words of Madonna, the queen of Pop: "Don't just stand there. Let's go to it. STRIKE A POSE There's nothing to it".

Lukas Feireiss

TRAMP

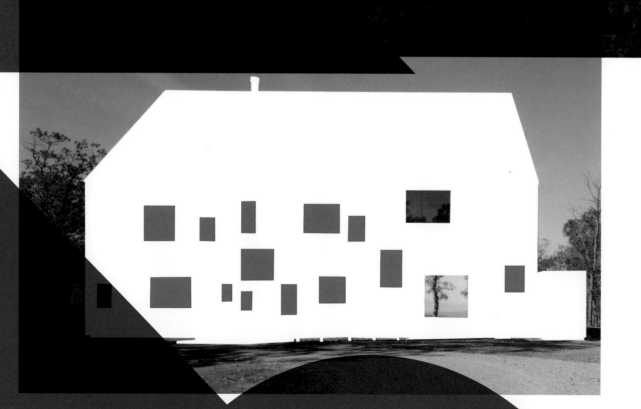

"WHAT YOU CALL ME? **TRAMP**. YOU DON'T WEAR CONTINENTAL CLOTHES, OR STETSON HATS. YOU'RE A TRAMP!" Otis Redding

The first chapter, Tramp, looks at eccentric stand-alone architectures situated away from the bustle of urban life that defy traditional building conventions and draw their inspiration from their natural surroundings. The resulting architecture is characterised by the interaction and mutual interrogation of the built and the organic, the refined and the unrefined, constituting original shapes and inspiring examples of a new contextual building intelligence.

TEZUKA ARCHITECTS
Takaharu and Yui Tezuka
www.tezuka-arch.com

Forest House
Nagano, Japan, 2004

This cottage by Takaharu and Yui Tezuka floats in the forest, its roof tilted to optimise views of the treetops. The wide opening window extending from top to bottom in the living room area offers a great forest panorama. The entire house exploits daylight to the maximum by means of glazed roof fittings.

JARMUND / VIGSNAES

www.jva.no

Triangle House
Nesodden, Norway, 2006

<u>01</u>

<u>02</u>

01. Ground floor plan
02. 1st floor plan

This house is situated to afford views over the
sea between the branches of the surrounding
pine-forest. The permitted aerial building lines
define the plan and even the heights of the roofline. While exterior views are framed singly by
the window openings, closely related to individual
spaces, the interior is treated in a more fluent
way, with overlapping sequences of space and
light in section and plan. This duality of focus
and flow is the theme of the building.

FAR / FROHN & ROJAS
www.f-a-r.net

Wall House
Santiago de Chile, Chile, 2007

This project is a design investigation into how the qualitative aspects of the wall, as a complex membrane, structure our social interactions and climatic relationships and enable specific ecologies to develop, as opposed to the general notion that our living environments can be properly described and designed "in plan". The project breaks down the "traditional" walls of a house into a series of four delaminated layers (concrete cave, stacked shelving, milky shell, soft skin) in between which the different spaces of the house slip. Each layer is characterized by very specific climatic, atmospheric, structural, material and functional properties and as a result becomes part of the intelligent hierarchy underlying this low-budget project: while the innermost zones host the most demanding areas (e.g. kitchen and bathroom), the house and its materials roughen up toward the outside. The building's most oustanding feature, an energy screen typically used in greenhouse construction, constitutes the outermost layer, creating not only diffused lighting and a comfortably climatised zone inside but also, through its folding and sometimes reflective, sometimes translucent surface, contributes to the cut diamond appearance of the structure.

Atelier for a Calligrapher
Jamanaski, Japan, 2004

The Atelier for a Calligrapher includes not only a large atelier space but a small villa as well. Situated on top of a hill, the client asked for a roof-top for a view of the adjacent rice fields. The building's tilted form also facilitates it's maintenance during the winter months, for the heat of the sunlight gained on the North wall melts the snow on the flat roof.

THAM & VIDEGARD
HANSSON ARCHITECTS
www.tvh.se

Archipelago House
Stockholm, Sweden, 2006

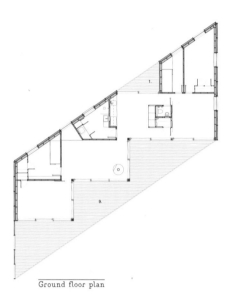

Ground floor plan

A.H. ARCHITECTS
Akira Hikone
www.a-h-a.architects.com

BOZ
Kanagawa, JAPAN, 2006

The starting point for this house is its direct relationship with the dramatic landscape, with the objective of offering within a simple frame - a platform - several
diverse readings of the space-nature relationship. Conceived as a lightweight construction in wood and glass, this summerhouse is located in the outer Stockholm
archipelago. The horizontal character of the black stained exterior relates to the ver-
ticals of tall, mature pines and the reflected views of the Baltic Sea. The geometry of
the plan is generated by the specifics of the site, the house being fitted into the flat
surface between two cliffs and turning simultaneously towards the sun on the south
side and frontally towards the sea on the west side. With the small rooms placed in
the back, the social areas of the house stand out as an open platform crisscrossed by
sliding glass. This zigzag layout also creates a series of outside spaces sheltered from
the strong winds.

BKK ARCHITECTS
Black Kosloff Knott Pty Ltd
www.b-k-k.com.au

Falvey House
Warburton, Australia, 2008

On an elevated site set amongst native bushland with rolling views to the north, the Wall House refuses to be seen as visitors approach, presenting a mute block wall embedded in the site. The wall forms a protective courtyard space with the existing topography, continuing BKK's interest in the relationship between building and landscape through a type of embedded occupation. The house then pursues our interest in the way in which a drawn line becomes a wall that acts to claim space or mark territory. Internally, spaces are organised and anchored by the wall, which unfolds as one moves through the house. A confined entry opens out to reveal panoramic views of mountains to the north.

01 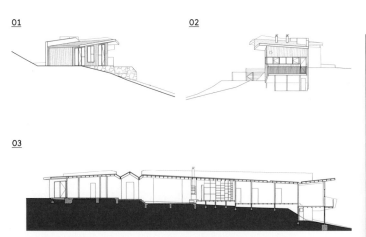 02

03

01. South-east elevation; 02. North-west elevation; 03. Longitudinal section

LAR / FERNANDO ROMERO
www.lar-fernandoromero.com

Ixtapa House
Punta Ixtapa, Mexico, 2001

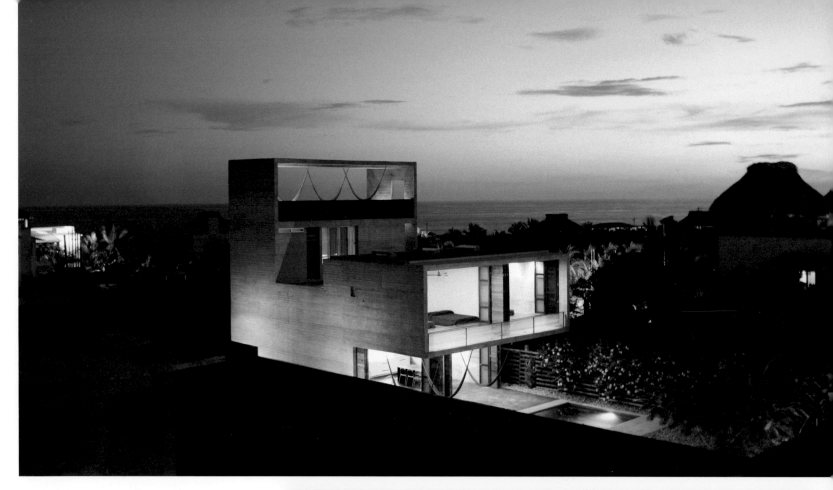

CADAVAL & SOLÀ-MORALES
Eduardo Cadaval and Clara Solà-Morales
www.ca-so.com

TDA House
Puerto Escondido, Mexico, 2006

Cadaval & Solà Morales's low-cost beach house requires minimum maintenance and is extremely flexible in its uses and configurations. The entire house can open up completely to the exterior or close in on itself. High temperatures, saltpeter, and an unskilled labour force were the conditions that persuaded the architects to built this house in concrete. The section of the house, with its pronounced cantilevers, tries to take to the limit the structural and tectonic qualities of the building material, but above all attempts to adapt the house to the specific conditions of its location. Three elements are defined for three different conditions: a tower volume which, in search of the sea, interrupts its opacity at strategic points until it achieves complete openness at the level where nothing blocks its views over the Mexican Pacific Ocean; a second bedroom volume suspended over the water and the wild flowers of the garden; and a third element built to be a wide, high, fresh central space which distributes and channels the different activities of the house. These three elements merge into a single volume of uncertain scale and rough textures.

KWK PROMES
www.kwkpromes.pl

Aatrial House
Lower Silesia, Poland, 2006

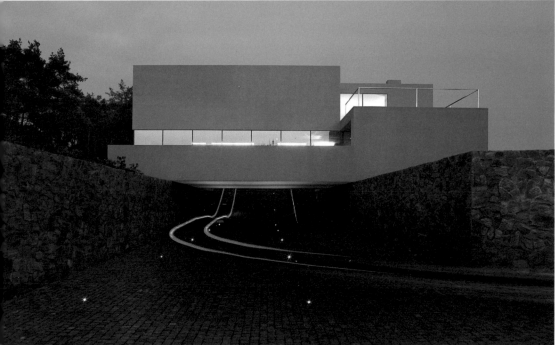

For this project in Lower Silesia, the driveway is pushed into the ground and leads into the ground floor level from underneath the building. As a result the building opens up onto all sides with its terraces in an unrestricted manner.

POWERHOUSE COMPANY
www.powerhouse-company.com

Villa 1
Ede, The Netherlands, 2007

Set in the woodlands of Holland, the programme of Villa 1 is optimally oriented towards views of the terrain, and the sun. Half of the programme is pushed below ground to meet local zoning regulations. This creates a clear dichotomy in the spatial experience of the house - a glass box ground floor where all the mass is concentrated in furniture elements, and a 'medieval' basement, where the spaces are carved out of the mass.

MEIXNER SCHLÜTER WENDT ARCHITEKTEN
www.meixner-schlueter-wendt.de

House Wohlfahrt-Laymann
Frankfurt, Germany, 2004

The Wohlfarht-Laymann House is situated in a relatively exclusive residential area in the Taunus outside Frankfurt am Main. A new shell was built around the original house, an archetypal wooden country cottage dating from the 1930s, thus creating a new interior and intermediate space. The position of the shell and its distance at different points from the inner house is dictated by the functional requirements of the ground plan structure. Paradoxes occur in the house, where an apparently normal reality becomes distorted and a simple, a traditional country cottage becomes a dream of cosmopolitan density in the suburbs.

This extraordinary example of ecologically sensitive building by Spanish architect Edduardo Arroyo of No.Mad Arquitectos is to be found in the woodlands near Spain's capital, Madrid. The Levene House ingeniously complies with the existing topography by developing its original architectural design without interfering with the site's dominant tree population. None of the existing trees has been cut down.

OFIS ARHITEKTI

www.ofis-a.si

Villa Old Oaks

Ljubljana, Slovenia, 2008

The residence is situated in a new neighbourhood with six large villas. The unique feature of the site is a splendid view of a stand of oak trees that are over a hundred years old. The terrain slopes down towards these trees. To guarantee that most of the major spaces will have access to this view, the house is organised on stepped levels following the terrain. The outline of the house keeps to the shape of the plot of land, minus four metres all around,

the minimum distance Slovenian law calls for vis-à-vis one's neighbours.

The heart of the house is an external covered courtyard. Main spaces such as the entrance lobby and staircase, the children's playroom, the dining, living, bedroom and work areas overlook this space. The staircase roof is glazed. The courtyard roof is part glass, part wood and has views of the sky and the treetops, thus creating a strong link between inside and outside.

01. Undeground floor plan; 02. Ground floor plan; 03. 1st floor plan

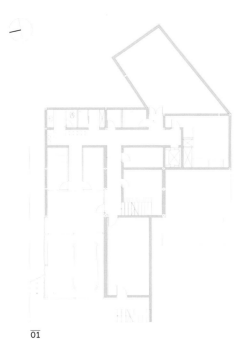

01

02

03

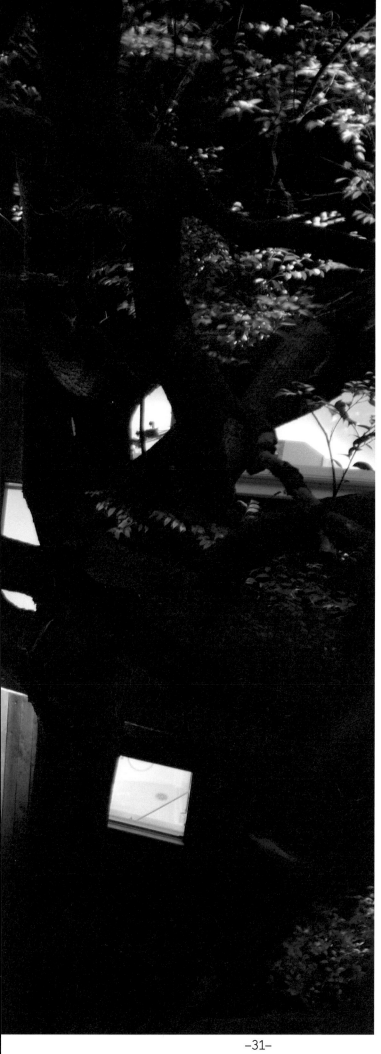

HIROSHI NAKAMURA & NAP ARCHITECTS
www.nakam.info

Dancing Trees, Singing Birds
Tokyo, Japan, 2006

This project by Hiroshi Nakamura & Nap Architects is another outstanding example of today's environmentally aware building practices. The building with its playful tree house appearance elaborately draws all the trees on site into the building's overall concept by simultaneously dodging and using them. All rooms are constructed so that they don't harm the existing tree population. In order to use the maximum space without cutting down the trees, every single branch was therefore measured by laser and the rooms were installed in spaces that are safe from the tree movements caused by typhoons - the powerful storm characteristic of Japan.

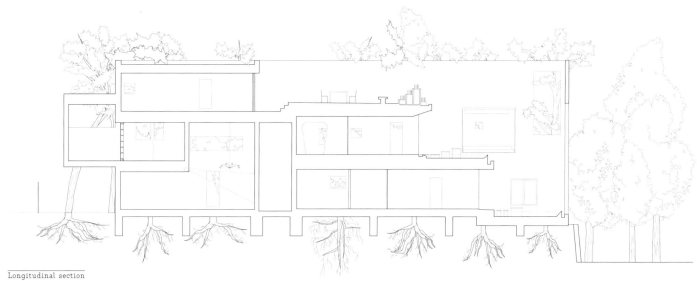

Longitudinal section

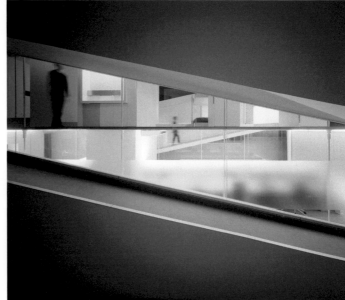

CURIOSITY INC.
www.curiosity.jp

C-2
Yamanashi, Japan, 2006

C-2 is a weekend house designed for a musician as a stage to enhance nature near Mount Fuji. The house is located on a very dramatic and difficult site, very steeply sloping land in the middle of a very dense forest of tall trees.

MEIXNER SCHLÜTER WENDT ARCHITEKTEN

www.meixner-schlueter-wendt.de

House F
Kronberg, Germany, 2007

The starting point for the planning of the house was the goal of coupling the residential quality and the topography of an idyllic orchard lawn with the living rooms of the house. An interesting debate ensues on the subject of pitched roofs, due to the stipulation of a pitched roof by the authorities and in relation to the individually designed roofs of the current and historical buildings in the neighbourhood,. The actual form is based on fundamental criteria such as function, construction, material, lighting etc. and associative form design. The associative ambivalent perception is, on the one hand, a dynamic, hovering vehicle or flying object, and on the other hand, a completely normal house with a pitched roof, built on a slope, where the mass of the garden floor has been subtracted. The garden floor is completely glazed, in order to connect the interior with the orchard lawn in an unbroken flow. Also in a flowing manner, the orchard lawn is furnished both inside and outside with boxes and spaces. The top storey appears to be a levitating body. The sheet-metal cladding echoes the ambivalence of roof and vehicle.

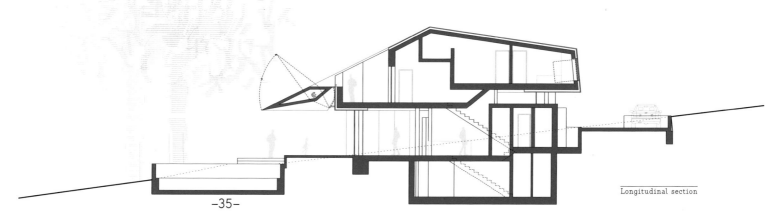

Longitudinal section

Tramp

CLOUD9
Enric Ruiz-Geli
www.e-cloud9.com

Villa Bio
Llers, Spain, 2004

The Villa Bio is conceived as landscape of linear events by the architect Enric Ruiz-Geli. A landscape that folds itself into the site and forms a growing spiral. The building's platform is a concrete C shape, constant in section. The longitudinal blind façades function as beams.

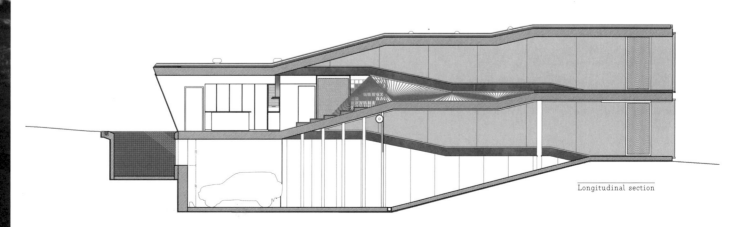

Longitudinal section

POTT ARCHITECTS
www.pottarchitects.com

House W
Berlin, Germany, 2005

House W is located in the former garden of a villa
built during the prosperous Gründerzeit years
in the late 19th century. The actual property is
accessed via its own lane, leading past the villa in
front. As it stands transverse to the access lane,
approaching visitors can look through a large
window straight into the central part of the house.
The entrance to the house is below ground level,
where there is a spacious foyer with a cloakroom
and service areas. Structurally the house is a
single volume, zoned by through wall and ceiling
elements. The arrangement of the rooms along two
parallel access corridors running from the study
in the east to the patio creates an enfilade effect
which can, where required, be extended or short-
ened by sliding doors.

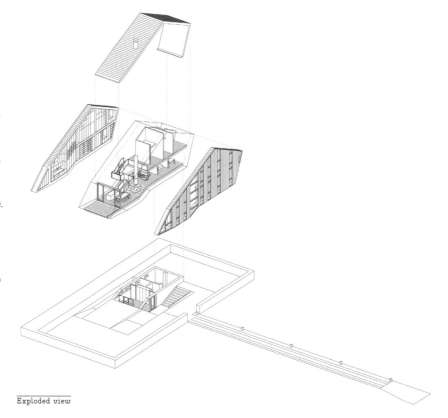

Exploded view

POTT ARCHITECTS

www.pottarchitects.com

House L
Berlin, Germany, 2006

BIEHLER WEITH ASSOCIATED
www.biehler-weith.de

House in Fichtestrasse
Heilbronn, Germany, 2007

The building is perched atop a hill gazing over the town of Heilbronn, with rolling vineyards leading the eye far into the distance. The statical impression given by the original cubic building from 1929 has been unified with new elements in a dynamic spatial design. The old brick-walled building has been newly clad with a composite thermal insulation system, its surface refined with a high-quality exterior plaster. In contrast, the new addition - constructed entirely from concrete - has drawn a dynamic thread through the previously existing edifice. In order to accentuate the vivid character of the new building, the architects chose aluminum sandwich panels to clad the façade.

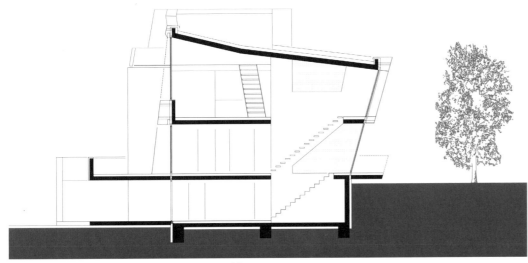

Longitudinal section

Tramp

COOP HIMMELB(L)AU
Wolf D. Prix
www.coop-himmelblau.at

Villa Soravia
Millstatt, Austria, 2006

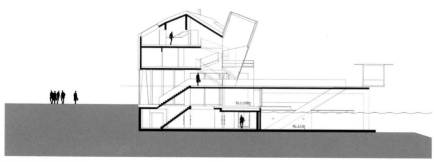
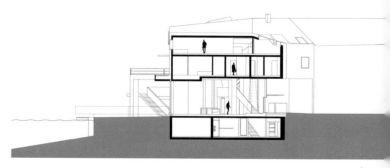

Longitudinal sections

Tramp

The Villa Soravia, a vacation home, is on the shore of Lake Mill-statt, at the southernmost tip of Millstatt, a health resort in Carinthia, Austria. COOP HIMMELB(L)AU realized the Soravia family's summer villa as a renovation project, since building regulations required that the contours of the previous structure and the angle of its roof be preserved. With these specifications, COOP HIMMELB(L)AU produced a vacation home, the form of which is defined by the original gable roof, a slanted tower, a generously designed exterior, and an inimitable spatial structure. The simple structural concrete, white painted wood and metal surfaces, and consciously anti-tectonic joint pattern of the Villa Soravia lend the home an atmosphere of ease and serenity. A terrace extends the living room out towards the lake at ground level.

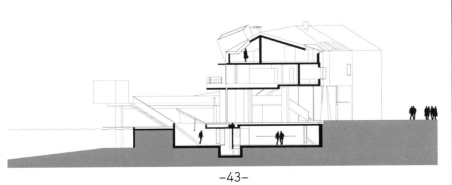

WOLFGANG TSCHAPELLER

St. Joseph
St. Joseph, Austria, 2007

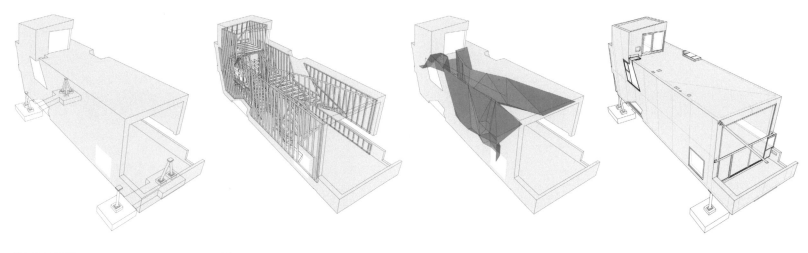

For this project, Wolfgang Tschapeller created a concrete form to be made habitable independent of the side of the building. The building's concrete shell is placed at the edge of an area remaining along the Danube floodplains. The concrete form is set on four supports – one one-legged element, two two-legged elements and one three-legged element that join to hold the building above the ground.

A second form, soft, white and independent of the outer shell, is set within the concrete outer covering. The white form opens up and programme the concrete shell's interior.

JARMUND / VIGSNÆS
www.jva.no

White House
Gimsøstraumen, Norway, 2006

Pull House
Vermont, USA, 2008

The house embraces local tradition by revising the barn prototype. A simple pitched roof "barn" has had one corner pulled out and moved diagonally from its rectangular loci. This folds the entry gable façade away from the ridge and creates a strong diagonal south façade. These simple distortions are juxtaposed with the north side of the building, which appears quite ordinary. From the gable ends one can see the building as a vernacular "saltbox" form or an extended roof with changed pitch, neither of which are true. The folded gable west entry façade is painted with a strong colour emphasis to accent its difference. The east and north façades are clad with rough timber coloured to look like old weathered "barn boards" with random openings. The roof is in vertical seamed metal, which is widely used locally.

The Goodman House contains a Dutch barn frame that has been transported and re-erected. The house looks as though it has been turned inside-out, as a passageway traverses the width of the whole interior space. Thermally transformable, the breezeway converts into a winter garden by means of slide-up screen doors and roll-down glass doors. The clients' affection for the antiquated timbers combined with their desire for a brightly lit and predominantly undivided interior did not allow for the reintroduction of the mezzanines and partitions that typically stabilise barn structures from within. Therefore, lateral structural stability has been reintroduced by a steel frame surrounding the barn. A curtain wall, with irregularly distributed windows, encloses the peripheral steel frame.

PRESTON SCOTT COHEN
www.pscohen.com

Goodman House
Dutchess County, USA, 2004

HUDSON ARCHITECTS
www.hudsonarchitects.co.uk

Cedar House
North Elmham, United Kingdom, 2005

MOS
www.mos-office.net

Terry Winters Studio
Taconik State Park, USA, 2007

This MOS practice project explores the idea of creating a space for both painting and drawing set against an intense landscape of shale cliffs, forest and ponds. Overlooking the hills of the Taconic State Park, this isolated site is one of several free-standing structures forming a compound for an artist and a curator/writer. Creating a space for both drawing and painting, in addition to providing for the amenities of storage, cooking, cleaning, and reading, posed the problem of how to achieve extreme openness in order to move freely between the media of painting and drawing. The design focuses on constructing an open space from painting to drawing uninterrupted by structure. This dictated the design of the structural system and permitted a column-free interior with moment frames on each end that would serve as external porches and viewing spaces between nature and the built environment.

DSDHA
www.dsdha.co.uk

St. Annes, Colchester Sure Start
Colchester, United Kingdom, 2006

The architects were commissioned to design the new Sure Start and community building to serve the St. Anne's area of Colchester. During the day the building is a base for specific services such as health clinics, parent support groups, crèche and playgroups. The centre is used for general community activities at the other times, evenings and weekends and the Soroptomists International have a base here too. An incubator unit provides office space for a small business start-up. The building's dynamic undulating form was designed using the analysis of views and movement on the site. The triangulated roof can be seen above the surrounding roads and green spaces, creating a local landmark and beacon.

JARMUND / VIGSNÆS

www.jva.no

Dønning Community Building

Gimsøstraumen, Norway, 2006

The old building for the Dønning Youth Society, an independent and local community organisation, burnt down a couple of years ago. Now the new building combines rest facilities and a café for tourists in the tourist season with a community building for the rest of the year. The site slopes towards the water. The vegetation is low, indicating the harsh local climatic conditions. The building stands on its own, not unlike the big rocks left from glacial activities you find scattering the Norwegian landscapes. The building is relatively closed, with the central communal space surrounded by supporting functions. The entrance appears almost as a big mouth, a clear cut, which reveals the interior. The large glass opening also provides contact with the midnight sun. The structure is designed to be as simple and cost efficient as possible. The exterior is covered in corrugated fiber cement boards. The large openings are covered in wooden panelling, painted bright red.

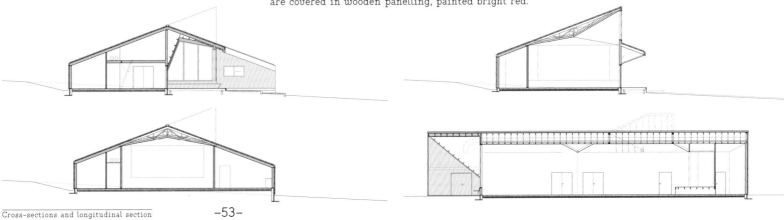

Cross-sections and longitudinal section

JARMUND / VIGSNÆS
www.jva.no

Svalbard Science Centre
Svalbard, Norway, 2005

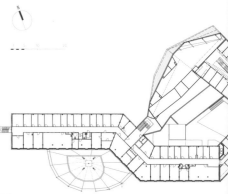

The project was commissioned through an invited competition. The new structure is an addition to an existing university and research building and provides new facilities for the Svalbard Museum. The insulated copper-clad skin is wrapped around the required programme creating an outer shell adjusted to the flows of wind and snow passing through the site. The building is elevated on poles to prevent the melting of the permanent frost – the only thing fixating the construction. The main structure is in timber, to facilitate on-site adjustments and avoid cold bridges. The outer copper cladding retains its workability even at low temperatures, thereby extending the construction period further into the cold season. An important consideration has been to create vital public spaces and passages in the building, an "interior campus" area providing warm and lighted meeting places during the dark and cold winter. The pine-clad spaces have complex geometry relating to the outer skin of the building; the effectiveness of the circulation is maximized but at the same time it offers varied vistas and experiences.

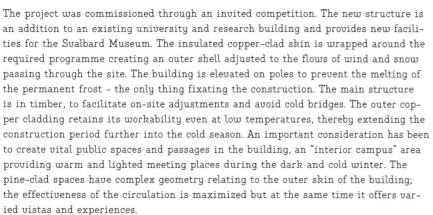

$\overline{02}$

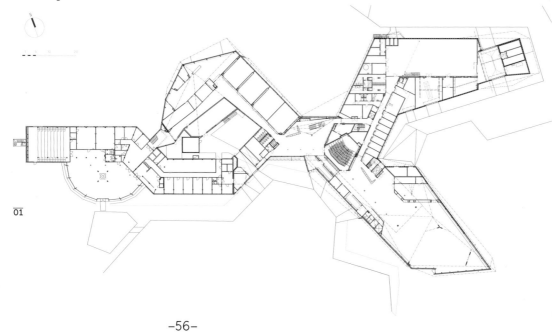

$\overline{01}$

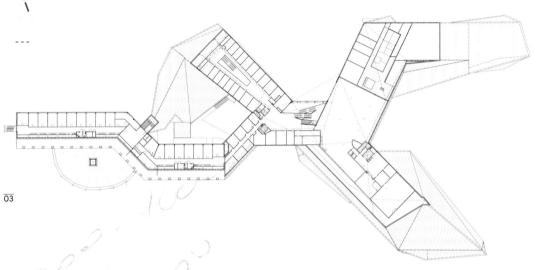

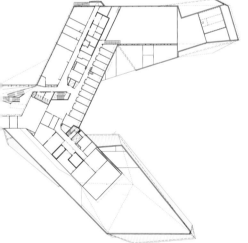

01. Ground floor plan
02. 1st floor plan
03. 2nd floor plan

The area around the village of Hinzert is an idyll in a German landscape characterised by rounded hills and agricultural land. No original traces identify its use between 1939 and 1945, when the site was a special camp for political prisoners from more than 20 countries. The prize-winning project by Wandel Hoefer Lorch + Hirsch addresses the political and territorial deformations of the landscape with a document center including archives, research library, seminar and exhibition spaces. The all-in-one structure, roof and façade consists of over three thousand different triangular plates of 12-millimeter Corten steel. The reddish brown envelope encases an elongated exhibition space, a seminar room, a library, an archive and offices, with sightlines giving the impression of a single spatial unit.

Around the central exhibition-archive space a series of 'pockets' containing archive units, large exhibits and small research cells push the volume outwards into the landscape. The inner skin consists of triangular birch plywood panels on which photographs and texts are inscribed by a direct printing process: documents are not applied to the building, but directly linked to it, like a contemporary form of fresco.

WANDEL HOEFER LORCH + HIRSCH
www.wandel-hoefer-lorch.de

The Hinzert Museum and Document Center
Hinzert, Germany, 2005

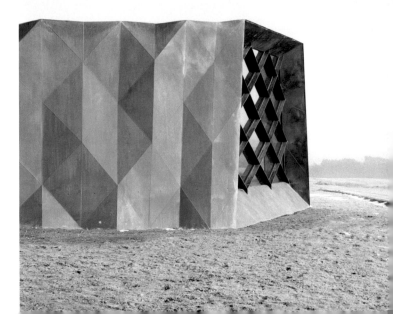

TATIANA BILBAO
www.tatianabilbao.com

Jinhua Pavilion
Jinhua Architecture Park, China, 2006

Longitudinal section

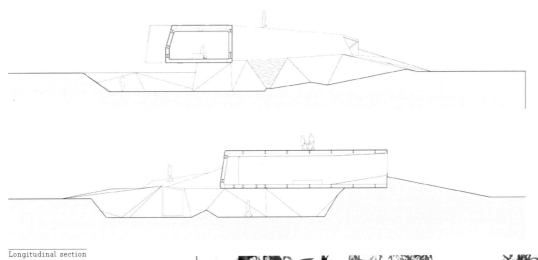

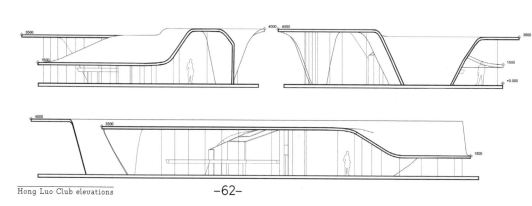

MAD OFFICE
www.i-mad.com

Hong Luo Club
Beijing, China, 2006

The Hong Luo Club House has two branches, one a swimming pool floating on the lake, the other an underwater platform. The architectural form is based on people's circulation. Two major roads converge at the centre of the house and extend all the way up along an ascending roof. The ever changing water surface joins the ascending roof, expressing the transition from liquid to solid. The building's spatial structure and the functions are integrated naturally. The main entrance to the house will take the visitor to 1.3 mm under water, where people feel they are walking in the lake. The access road ascends to ground level gradually as it nears the house, thus revealing the main function of the building -- a gathering space. The roof shape is a projection of the linear, functional organisation of the ground level programme. The outdoor swimming pool is built into the lake, keeping the surfaces of the natural and the artificial water at the same level.

Hong Luo Club elevations

TOMMIE WILHELMSEN
www.tommie-wilhelmsen.no

Villa Hellearmen
Stavanger, Norway, 2005

This private family house located at Hafrsfjord, on the south east coast of Norway aims mainly to break out of the predictable sameness of typical Scandinavian suburbia. The most important room in the house is the garden. Outside and inside are not two separate phenomena in this house. The ambition is to bring the typical light of each Scandinavian season into the house, but also to bring the house out into the garden.

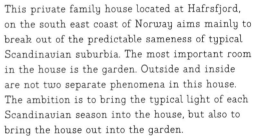

BIG/ BJARKE INGELS GROUP
www.big.dk

MAR / Maritime Youth House
Copenhagen, Denmark, 2004

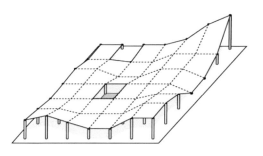

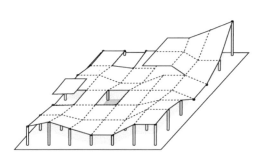

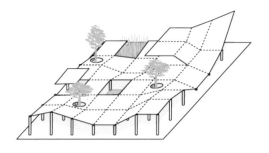

Grid diagrams

Two very different users share the facilities of this public land-scape of social funtions: a sailing club and a youth centre with conflicting requirements: the youth centre wanted outdoor space for the kids to play; the sailing club required most of the site to moor their boats. The building is the result of these two contradictory demands: the deck is elevated high enough to allow for boat storage underneath while providing an undulating landscape for the kids to run and play above.

The project involves an extension of a 19th-century villa located in a beautiful Alpine resort by Lake Bled. Both the old villa and the landscape were strictly regulated by the National Heritage authority. The client's chief request was for the main living area to be twice the size of the old existing villa. On top of that, most of the spaces had to face the lake. Ofis Arhitekti's proposal placed new spaces beneath the ground floor of the existing villa. The extension forms a rounded base around the house – a pillow covered by the landscape. Looking from the other side of the lake, the pillow blurs with the surrounding landscape. The elevation under the pillow is glazed and overlooks the lake. The main entrance is from the courtyard and is shifted off the house's central axis; you enter the side volume of the old villa cellar, in the new section. Then you crosse the curved ramp and pass beneath the staircase. Here, a three-storey hall opens up to form the heart of the old villa, while the visual axis of the lake conducts you to the new living area.

The curved stairs define the space, connect the old and the new, and act as the main communications core in the house. All rooms and open spaces give onto the staircase and communicate with the main lobby.

OFIS ARHITEKTI
www.ofis-a.si

Villa "Under" Extension
Bled, Slovenia, 2004

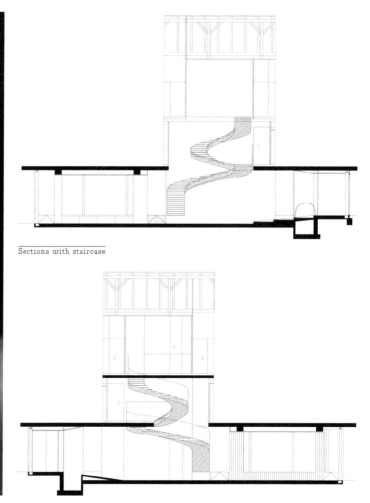

Sections with staircase

—67—

Tramp

ZAHA HADID ARCHITECTS
www.zaha-hadid.com

Nordpark Cable Railway
Innsbruck, Austria, 2007

PAUL ANDREU
www.paul-andreu.com

The National Grand Theatre of China
Beijing, China, 2007

The Beijing National Grand Theatre is situated in the heart of Beijing on Chang An Avenue. The curved building, with a total surface area of 149,500 square meters, emerges like an island in the centre of a lake. The titanium shell is in the shape of a super ellipsoid. It is divided in two by a curved glass covering. During the day, light flows through the glass roof into the building. At night, movements within can be seen from outside. The building houses three performance auditoriums – an opera house, a concert hall and a theatre – as well as art and exhibition spaces open to a wide public and integrated into the city. The building is connected to the shore by a transparent underpass. This entrance leaves the exterior of the building intact, without any openings, and mysterious looking, while providing the public with a passage from their daily world to the world of opera, fiction and dreams.

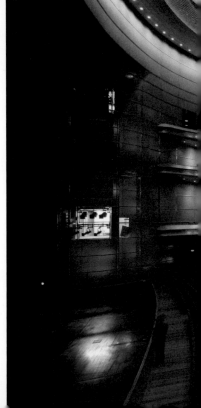

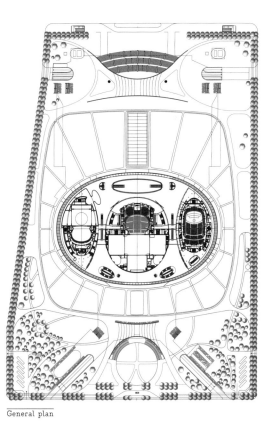

General plan

MASS STUDIES
www.massstudies.com

Ann Demeulemeester Shop
Seoul, Korea, 2007

The site is located in an alley, a block away from
Dosandae-ro, a busy thoroughfare in Seoul's
Gangnam district, very near Dosan Park. Primarily residential in the past, the neighbourhood
is undergoing a rapid transformation into an
upscaled commercial district full of shops and
restaurants. The building has one bsaement level
and three floors above. The Ann Demeulemeester
Shop is located on the first floor, with a restaurant above and a Multi-Shop in the basement.
This proposal is an attempt to incorporate as
much nature as possible into the building within
the constraints of a low-elevation, high-density
urban environment with limited space. The
building defines its relationship between natural/
artificial and interior/exterior as an amalgamation, rather than a confrontation.

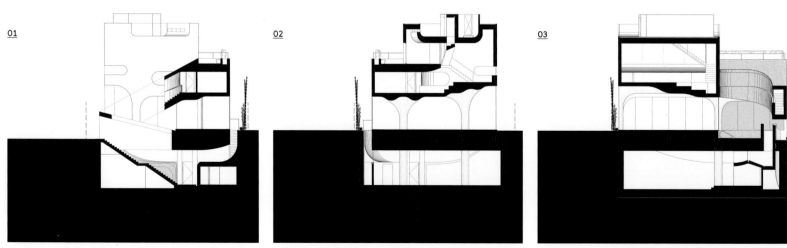

01   02   03

<u>01. + 02.</u> Cross-section; <u>03.</u> Longitudinal section

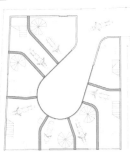

01

01. Ground floor plan
02. 1st floor plan
03. 2nd floor plan

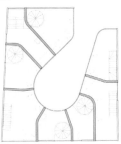

02

03

YUJI NAKAE
AKIYOSHI TAKAGI
HIROFUMI OHNO

www.nakae-a.jp; www.at-a.net; www.ohno-japan.com

Ne Apartment
Tokyo, Japan, 2007

This 8-unit rental apartment house complex was designed to house motorcycle enthusiasts in Tokyo, with a built-in garage included in every unit. The building is located on a flag-shaped plot near the apex of a triangular block, with a certain degree of open space facing the main road to the south. The c-shaped design was a practical decision to allow the residents to access their apartments through a common alley that leads right to the center of the complex. The resulting little square avoids giving the impression of a narrow and dark dead end, and allows the residents to turn their bikes easily.

–75–

y model

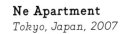

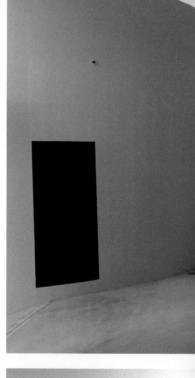

KATSUHIRO MIYAMOTO & ASSOCIATES
www.kmaa.jp

Clover House
Nishinomiya-City, Japan, 2006

For the Clover House, a housing development site and the existing retaining wall were excavated to create double-height space in the basement, and, in addition, a flat glass box was layered on the ground to house the living accommodation.

–76–

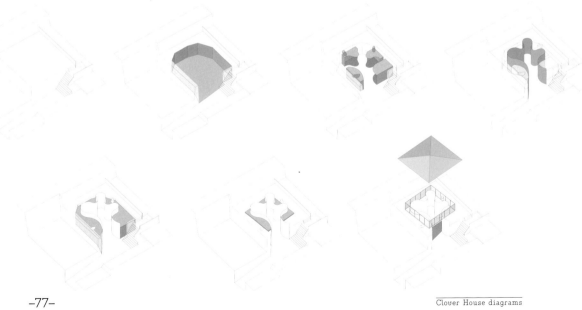

Clover House diagrams

3DELUXE
www.3deluxe.de

Leonardo Glass Cube
Bad Driburg, Germany, 2007

The exhibition pavilion with conference rooms for a high-grade glass and gift article brand is the first permanent building realised by 3deluxe. The open floor plan layout of the clearly designed and multi-functional Leonardo building enables an integrative linkage of product presentation zones, seminar and meeting rooms, inspiring work areas and a lot more besides. The building consists essentially of two formally contrasting elements: a geometrically stringent, cube-like shell volume and a free form positioned centrally in the interior. The curved white wall encloses an introverted exhibition space and its other side circumscribes the extroverted hallway along the glass façade.

–78–

NETZWERK ARCHITECTEN
www.netzwerk-architekten.de

Protestant Thomas Parish Centre
Mannheim, Germany, 2007

The new Protestant parish centre is a one-storey building with a square outline. The roof has greenery planted on it and an oval green yard with the foyer, hall, group rooms and roofed event areas set around it. What emerges is a U shaped ground plan configuration with two interior wings and a roofed exterior wing. The typology of the square building, which is linked with a new connecting passage for public use on the north side of the building, places the parish centre in the middle of a spacious public urban area. While the façade on the inner yard is constructed as a glassy curtain which can be opened in sections, the exterior cutting edges of the square are designed as a sculptural structure made of prefabricated concrete pieces with filigree perforations. Alongside the adjacent urban area, this structure surrounds the glazed building without delimiting it - it expresses the openness of the parish.

JÜRGEN MAYER H.
www.jmayerh.com

Dupli.Casa
Ludwigsburg, Germany, 2008

The geometry of the building is based on the footprint of the house previously located on the site. Originally built in 1984 and with many extensions and modifications since then, the new building echoes "family archaeology" by duplication and rotation. Lifted up, it creates a semi-public space on ground level between two discrete layers. The skin of the villa creates a sophisticated connection between inside and outside and offers spectacular views over the old town of Marbach and the German national literature archive on the other side of the Neckar valley

NEIL M. DENARI ARCHITECTS
www.nmda-inc.com

Alan-Voo House
Los Angeles, USA, 2007

When renovating and extending this existing family building, Neil M. Denari Architects kept half of the house for the children's bedrooms and incorporated the other half plus new extensions at the front and back into a public zone and a private bedroom for the parents. This strategy amounts to a new linear house being inserted into the existing house. Multi-toned, bright colors accentuate the new sections, suggesting a graphic expression representing the family's interests.

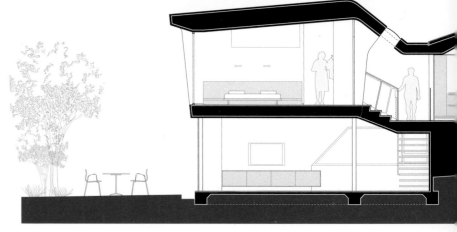

–82–

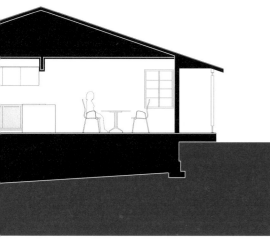

Longitudinal section

TONY OWEN NDM
www.tondm.com.au

Harley Davidson Headquarters
Sydney, Australia, 2007

TONDM have created the new Harley Davidson headquarters as part of the new West Lane Cove business park. The building has been designed as an iconic gateway to the site. The brief for the building is a reflection of the Harley Davidson culture, giving as much emphasis to the gymnasium and break areas as the office and storage space. The architects tried to reflect this by locating all the recreational areas near the entrance.

ABSTRACT PLANE

"I COULD SIT ON THE ROOF ON TOP OF THAT ABSTRACT HOUSE, SEE MY ABSTRACT VIEW, AN ABSTRACT MOUSE. I WANT TO LIVE ON AN **ABSTRACT PLANE.**" Frank Black

The projects in the Abstract Plane chapter are located within the urban context and vividly illustrate the creative richness that emerges when thinking out of the box. The examples here range from private residences to public buildings, opera houses and museums – to mention only a few. In their formal vocabulary they move from minimalistic to ever more complex styles, appropriately conveying an impression of the diverse language of architectural forms today.

SANAA
Kazuyo Seijima and Ryue Nishizawa
www.sanaa.co.jp

New Museum of Contemporary Art
New York, USA, 2007

The New Museum, designed by Tokyo-based architects Kazuyo Sejima and Ryue Nishizawa/SANAA, is a seven-storey structure on the Bowery in New York City. The first art museum ever constructed from scratch in downtown Manhattan, the New Museum opened to the public on December 1, 2007, coinciding with the institution's 30th anniversary. The New Museum building is a home for contemporary art and an incubator for new ideas, as well as an architectural contribution to New York's urban landscape. The seven-storey composition - a stack of rectangular boxes shifted off axis in different directions, clad in silvery galvanised, zinc-plated steel, and punctuated by skylights and windows offering vistas and vignettes of the city - doubles the size of the New Museum's former facilities on Broadway in Soho. In addition to dramatically expanded, flexible and column-free exhibition space, the building offers an innovative new media centre, a black-box theatre/auditorium, bookstore, expanded classrooms, library and study centre, café, and wrap-around rooftop terraces. At night, the building's metallic exterior will be washed with artificial lighting from within.

Double Window House
Tokyo, Japan, 2005

A.H. ARCHITECTS
Akira Hikone
www.a-h-architects.com

AIN House
Tokyo, Japan, 2003

The project is a house for the family of four situated in a hilly residential area. It was planned as a single storey house with a relaxing and warm atmosphere. The site is raised above street level, where the parking area is. The peripheral zone of the building is raised on five independent concrete frames. The steel beams suspended from the concrete are from a simple rectangular shape, which supports the floating part firmly. As the living room is placed at the centre of the building, the bedrooms, kitchen and dining room are in the peripheral zone. The living room, with higher ceiling and lower floor, is the space for gathering and circulating. Although the concrete frames could be seen as the boundary, they do not separate the rooms completely because of the transparent glass near the ceiling. Frames create a certain privacy and certain distance in this continuously flowing space. Although the building has rather a quiet image from outside, there are open and bright spaces inside.

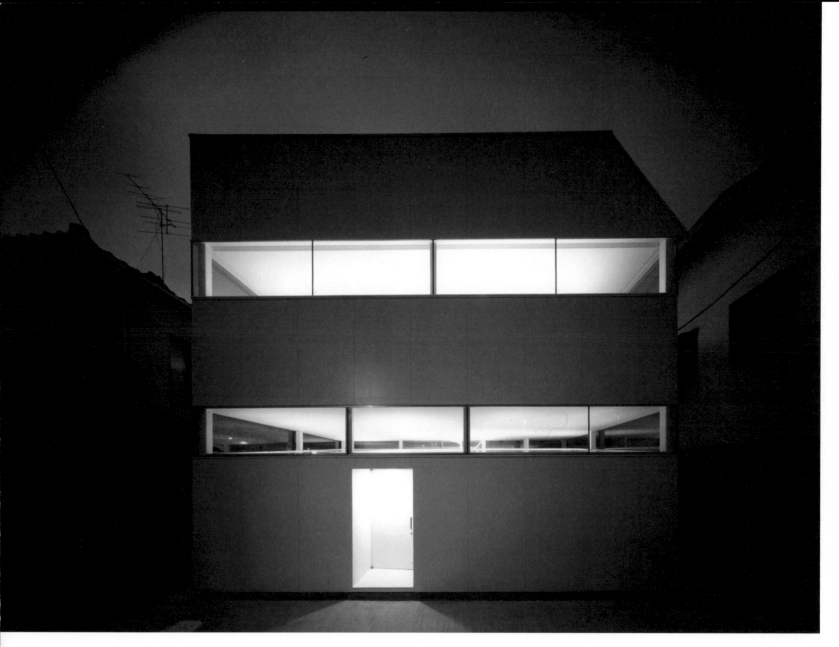

**KIYONOBU NAKAGAME ARCHITECT
& ASSOCIATES**
www.nakagame.com/

House in Kichijoji
Tokyo, Japan, 2005

The basic architectural design for the C-1 project, a glass box surrounded by a walkway-gallery that connects the floors, was designed before the site was found. The design is shaped from a user's point of view, with movement and discovery as the main theme. As the walkway surrounds the house, the interior is designed in 3 dimensions, visible from floor level to ceiling level. The top of a table is as visible as the bottom.

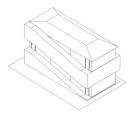

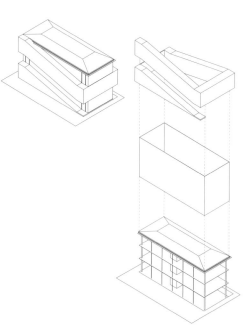

Axometry

KLEIN DYTHAM ARCHITECTURE
www.klein-dytham.com

Sin Den
Tokyo, Japan, 2007

The Sin Den house, with its characteristic graphic images on the outside of a massive black box,
was built for a young couple and a baby, providing
accommodation for the family and their hairdress-
ing salon, on a 50 square meter site.

ALPHAVILLE
www.a-ville.net

PH Gallery 176
Tokyo, Japan, 2005

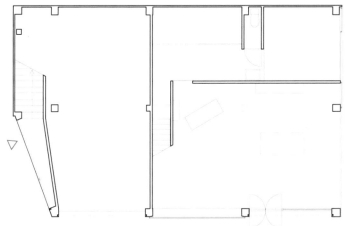

Ground floor plan

Abstract Plane

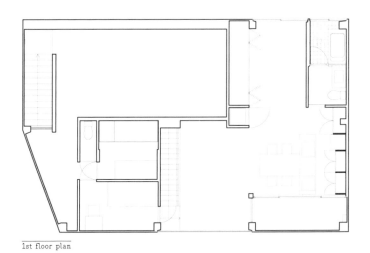
1st floor plan

ISAY WEINFELD
www.isayweinfeld.com

Livraria da Vila
Sao Paulo, Brazil, 2007

One enters the Livraria da Vila designed by Brazilian architect Isay
Weinfeld between pivoting bookshelves encased in glass—part door,
part window, part bookcase—that span the full width of the store.
When the cases are closed, one sees nothing but books from outside. When they are swung open, one still sees nothing but books,
because inside the walls are lined floor-to-ceiling with shelves, all
of them filled to capacity.

PETER GRUNDMANN

www.petergrundmann.com

House Neumann
Neubrandenburg, Germany, 2008

The house was built for a single woman and her son. Seven meters long, just under five meters wide, the house is vertically oriented through three storeys. A six meter-high concrete body sits four meters above ground, framing the floors to create a maximum amount of surface space. The ground level of the house is clad in wire and creates a light, atmospheric space. The wire also functions as protection for the staircase, a body of opaque, acrylic material that allows glimpses of the outside as well as of the inside to be seen through it as moving shadows and colours. The lot remains a public place, as people can walk under the house when passing and visually sense the house through its transparency. The empty lot will not be filled, but is given a new spatial quality that only accentuates its character and position in the urban context.

Abstract Plane

House Dagobertstrasse
Cologne, Germany, 2004

Abstract Plane

NKS ARCHITECTS
www.nksarc.com

3 Bundled Tubes
Tokyo, Japan, 2004

Abstract Plane

NARCHITECTS
www.narchitects.com

Switch Building
New York, USA, 2007

Switch Building is a 7-storey apartment and art gallery building
on the Lower East Side, New York City. The building consists of
four through apartments, a duplex penthouse, and a double height
art gallery on the ground and cellar levels. nArchitects provided
full architectural services for the project, including all interior
design. The project's design emerges from a creative interpretation
of some of the tight constraints imposed by zoning and the devel-
oper's needs. The "switching" concept opportunistically maximises
difference while maintaining the efficiencies of repetition. In a
reinterpretation of a bay window, an angled front facade switches
back and forth, allowing each through apartment unique views up
and down Norfolk Street and creating subtle variations in shadows
and reflections. From the inside, the bay windows provide deep
window seats surrounded by warm hardwood. At the rear of each
apartment, the living space extends out to large balconies, which
also shift from side to side, creating double-height spaces between
balconies to maximize afternoon light and neighbourly interactions.

-106-

Abstract Plane

LOT-EK
www.lot-ek.com

Sanlitun North Site / West Building
Beijing, China, 2008

Sanlitun North is located in Sanlitun, one of the neighbourhoods in central Beijing that are undergoing fast and radical transformation. It is part of a large commercial development with a master plan by Kengo Kuma, developed within a larger governmental aim to retrofit the Chinese capital with retail and office space. LOT-EK's building defines the entire west side of this new public urban space. The building houses primarily high-end retail on the lower levels along with restaurants and office suites on the higher floors. Facing the pedestrian piazza, the building elevation is conceived as a three-dimensional billboard to be filled with the future retail tenants' graphics and logos; its articulation relates to the trajectories of pedestrian movement and views through the landscape of the piazza and its surrounding buildings. Denoting a building under construction, a layer of blue metal mesh, supported by a cantilevered scaffolding-like structure, wraps around the entire building. Offset from the building, the mesh acts as a second skin buffering the city noise level and filtering direct sunlight for energy efficiency.

KSV KRÜGER SCHUBERTH VANDREIKE
www.ksv-network.de

Museum of Modern and Contemporary Art
Bolzano, Italy, 2008

A closed metal hull covers the elongated cube of the museum; in contrast, its ends open as transparent storefronts and serve as projection surfaces towards the city and the landscape. The building connects the city centre with the Talfer meadows and the landscape, rather like a large tube. The interior of the museum with its exhibition levels, library, education department, shop, and information centre can be seen from outside via the glazed entry façade. The retracted ends, protected by cantilevered building elements, allow use as a stage area and forum for events in the entry plaza and/or the riverside meadows. The museum bridges, as projected continuations of the foyer of the new museum, create a new connection between the historic city and the city quarters located to the west across the river Talfer.

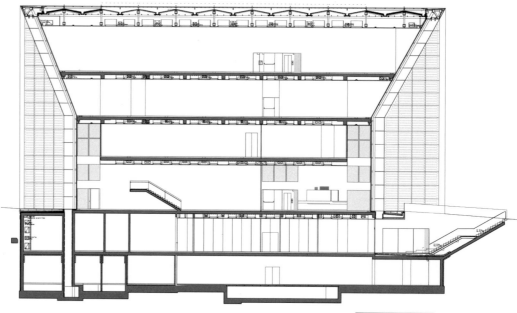

Longitudinal section

–108–

KLEIN DYTHAM ARCHITECTURE
www.klein-dytham.com

R3 Ukishima / aicafe54
Okinawa, Japan, 2007

Ai Café, a four unit commercial building, is located just off Koku-
sai Dori, the main tourist street in Naha, capital of Okinawa. The
building encloses a 25 meter-long, 5 meter-high perforated concrete
block screen which encloses a balcony access to the 2nd floor while
screening off a convenience store, electricity and telephone wires
running along the street. The screen with its pixelated pink orchid
pattern creates an internal world for the café while letting air and
light into the building. A four-storey tower at one end of the building can be seen from far away.

FASHION ARCHITECTURE TASTE
www.fashionarchitecturetaste.com

Blue House
London, United Kingdom, 2004

The Blue House by London-based FAT has a cartoon-like billboard character which communicates its function as a home and office. The front is on a miniature scale, but the side addressing the main street is large-scale. The project makes innovative use of standard construction methods. The house contains a maisonette for a family of three, an office and a separate apartment.

HERZOG & DE MEURON

CaixaForum Madrid
Madrid, Spain, 2008

The CaixaForum is conceived as an urban magnet, attracting not only art-lovers but everyone in Madrid and visitors from outside as well. This is due not only to the CaixaForum's cultural programme, but also to the building itself, insofar that its heavy mass is detached from the ground in apparent defiance of the laws of gravity and, in a real sense, draw the visitors inside. This new address for the arts is located in an area occupied until now by unspectacular urban structures. »

PLAZA DE LAS L

The classified brick walls of a former power station are reminiscences of the early industrial age
in Madrid, and a solitary gas station on site was
also clearly out of place. In order to conceive and
insert the new architectural components of the
CaixaForum Project into the converted power station, the architects began with a surgical opera-
tion, separating and removing the base and the
parts of the building that were no longer needed.
Separating the structure from the ground level
creates two worlds: one below and the other above
the ground. The "underworld" buried beneath the
topographically landscaped plaza provides space
for a theatre/auditorium, service rooms, and
several parking spaces. The multi-storey building above ground level houses the entrance lobby
and galleries, a restaurant and administrative
offices. The surprising sculptural aspect of the
CaixaForum's silhouette is no mere architectural
fancy, but reflects the roofscape of the surrounding buildings.

BÖGE LINDNER ARCHITEKTEN
www.boegelindner.de

Fire Practice House
Gelsenkirchen, Germany, 2005

Standing in front of a fire station, the Brandübungshaus – or, literally, "fire practice house" – enables the firemen to train in realistic conditions. The monolithic structure is built of reinforced concrete and Corten steel to withstand extremely high temperatures. The building is the architect's take on a pitched-roofed, single-family house, although its form has been stylised to add something like an architectural symbol to the understated glass-and-steel fire station. The house contains a kitchen, bedroom, living room and basement, all with mock furniture made of stainless steel.

ADAMO-FAIDEN
www.adamo-faiden.com.ar

Casas Lago
Buenos Aires, Argentine, 2007

The Casas Lago by the young Argentinian architects
Sebastián Adamo and Marcelo Faiden combine two economical
houses in a typical Buenos Aires neighbourhood.

AOKI JUN
www.aokijun.com

House A
Tokyo, Japan, 2007

YUKIO ASARI
YUJI NAKAE
HIROFUMI OHNO

www.lovearchitecture.co.jp; www.nakae-a.jp; www.ohno-japan.com

MG QUARTET
Tokyo, Japan, 2006

ARCHITECTURE-LAB
Shigekazu Takayasu and Syuhei Imazu
www.architecure-lab.com

House*4
Tokyo, Japan, 2006

Abstract Plane

AOKI JUN
www.aokijun.com

House G
Tokyo, Japan, 2004

Aoki Jun's G House is a contemporary abstraction of a traditional timber-framed house with a pitched roof. Situated in a residential district of central Tokyo, G House is a rendered house set on top of a reinforced concrete podium. With no distinction between wall and roof, the attic interior has a complex arrangement of interlocking spaces, lit by irregularly positioned skylights.

The Sagaponac House is a prototype weekend house designed for a wooded lot in Eastern Long Island. One of a number of houses commissioned for a new residential development, this project is characterised by its compact footprint and open interior spaces. The active roofline and wood cladding recall vernacular traditions, while the open floor plan and interlocking of solid and void acknowledge contemporary, informal lifestyles. The design of the house responds to site and climate through the use of local materials and careful solar orientation. On the south and west façades, there are minimal openings to prevent heat gain, while ample daylight from the skylights minimises the use of artificial light. This ensures that there will always be at least two natural light sources in every space in the house. Recycled materials were used wherever possible. Filtered, ambient light that changes with the seasons and time of day fills the house from the roof lights and window walls.

STAN ALLEN ARCHITECTS
www.stanallenarchitect.com

Sagaponac House
South Hampton, USA, 2006

BEHET BONDZIO LIN
www.2bxl.com

Guest House Jping
Taichung, Taiwan, 2001

Abstract Plane

This project in Brazil by London based Procter-Rihl was conceived as a slice built on an urban remnant left over after the opening of a new road on the west side of the site. Space is defined by a series of non-orthogonal design decisions. The space folds and unfolds within the prismatic form. It develops a series of spatial distortions, which create an illusion of greater space on this narrow plot. Entering at the narrow end, most of the site is a continuous open space for the social areas and inner courtyard.

PROCTER-RIHL
www.procter-rihl.com

Slice House
Sao Paolo, Brazil, 2004

PÉRIPHÉRIQUES ARCHITECTES
www.peripheriques-architectes.com

Banlieues Bleues
Patin, France, 2005

Within an urban industrial enclave in a dense suburban city centre, the "Banlieues Bleues" complex will be dedicated to contemporary music and its promotion. After the demolition of a few dilapidated buildings, the architects chose to keep its big old workshop hall in order to create a nave at the centre of the musical activities. The concert hall and the group of functions attached to the original industrial building are located in a new and autonomous building shaped like a prism. This building is inspired by big timber barns, but was distorted to adapt to the created garden geometry. As a result, the building is alive in its dynamics, and looks as if it is moving, "transformed by the sound of music". The offices and rehearsal studios are created in a long volume "en porte-à-faux", covered with golden scales, as "built in" in the nave. The coffee shop supporting a rehearsal studio is finished completely in glass, thus adding to the user-friendly character of the nave. As an interior micro urban space, the nave links all sections.

-125-

Abstract Plane

Flag-shaped sites have become rather common recently in Japan, especially in central urban areas - whether as a result of inheritance tax problems or real estate business ideas. The site of this building is tightly surrounded by its neighbours' walls, and not enough natural lighting is available from the side walls. Composing the architecture from the interior, the architects build up walls on lines offset by the appropriate distance from the lot borders . The floors are laid out freely in a large volume on four levels and loosely link the spaces in plan and section.

NAYA ARCHITECTS   **House in Futakosinchi**
Tokyo, Japan, 2004

KATSUHIRO MIYAMOTO & ASSOCIATES
www.kmaa.jp

Grappa
Takarazuka-City, Japan, 2006

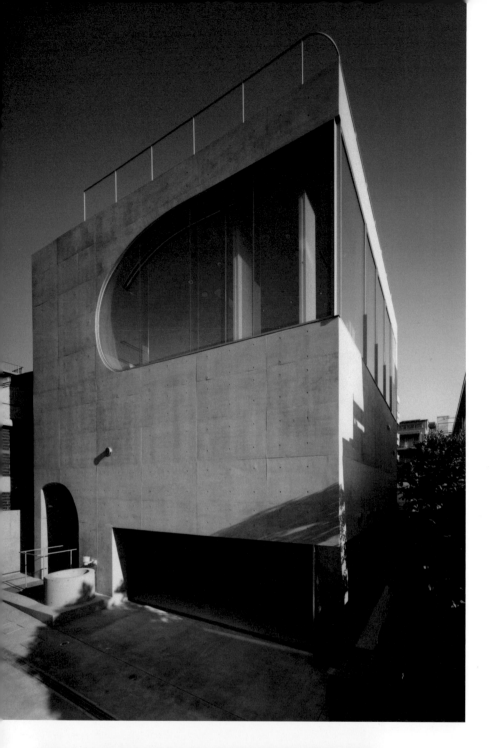

N MAEDA ATELIER
www5a.biglobe.ne.jp

The Rose
Tokyo, Japan, 2003

↳opposite pages
Flamingo
Tokyo, Japan, 2000

This powerful project by Norisada Maeda abolishes the notion of inside and outside by scooping three volumes out of one building block.

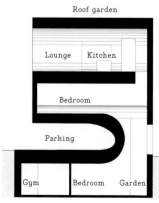
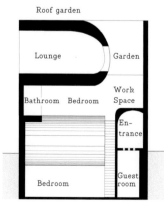

The Rose. Cross-section

The Flamingo project by the Japanese N Maeda Atelier is a pair
of small structures, rising in a lively city environment between a
national highway and an elevated railway. Cross-sectional C-shaped
frames, which differ slightly in the vertical direction, constitute
the floors to serve as living space, but also generate openings and
vaulted ceilings. Due to the extraordinarily small floor area, "passing points" such as the stairwell are also used as the bath, lavatory,
study, and so forth. While the project may be astonishingly small,
its naked frame appears to stand tall and unyielding in the throes
of the surrounding urban ugliness.

KATSUHIRO MIYAMOTO
& ASSOCIATES

www.kmaa.jp

Ship
Nishinomiya-City, Japan, 2006

This residence is built on a two-tiered site with a level difference of 3 meters. Because there were residual concerns about the credibility of an embankment, and about retaining the wall built along the housing development, the foundations were laid on natural ground beneath the lower tier that was more reliable as the supporting stratum. The steel volume for public rooms floats over the retaining wall and above the upper tier for a better view. Private rooms are arranged along the lower tier where the atmosphere is calm, at a distance from the front road, within a reinforced concrete structure which functions as a counterbalance to the overhanging volume. An optimal use of curved surfaces designed in response to the site's L-shaped plan was adopted in order to support the large cantilevered volume effectively.

NICHOLAS RAY & PLASTIK ARCHITECTS
www.nrap.co.uk

Gravesend Toilets
Gravesend, United Kingdom, 2007

ALPHAVILLE
www.a-ville.net

Hall House 1
Tokyo, Japan,

TERADADESIGN ARCHITECTS
Naoki Terada
www.teradadesign.com

T- Stomach House
Sitama, Japan, 2006

T-Stomach is an extraordinary house for a family with two children in the outskirts of Tokyo. This private residence stands out because of its courageous experiments in colour, shape and materials, experiencing the effect of natural sunlight mixed with paint colours as well as the enhancement of space with glossy and matt surfaces. The brief was to provide a house where the whole family can always be together. Therefore the house was designed as one fluid space, where the different living functions were laid out in a sequence. To fit on the site, the functions were squeezed, bent around a courtyard, and curved as a winding tube to resemble the confinement and twisting of the organs in a human body, while still allowing a sense of distance between the family members.

Abstract Plane

KIYONOBU NAKAGAME
ARCHITECT & ASSOCIATES
www.nakagame.com

House in Mitsuike
Yokohama, Japan, 2007

FUMITA DESIGN OFFICE INC.
www.fumitadesign.com

Nissan Grandrive
Yokosuka-shi, Japan, 2007

PÉRIPHÉRIQUES ARCHITECTES
www.peripheriques-architectes.com

L' Autre Canal / Regional Centre for Contemporary Music
Nancy, France, 2007

Abstract Plane

01. Longitudinal section; 02. Cross-section

HERTL ARCHITEKTEN
www.hertl-architekten.com

Ecker Abu Zahra House
Luftenberg, Austria, 2006

The house - for a teacher and a sociologist who
also keeps bees - is a simple cuboid with a square
ground plan. It is clad in copper plate, leaving
openings responding to the views. The most powerful of these is the one facing the almost baroque
natural parkway and connecting the living room
of the house with the garden at the highest point.
Inside, this space is defined by rooms arranged as
an L-shape on two floors. The hall itself is almost
six metres high. On the ground floor, the library,
a guest room and the apiculture about it; on the
upper floor there are bedrooms and bathrooms, a
workroom and a rooftop terrace.

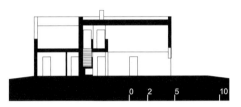

02

EM2N
www.em2n.ch

Theater 11
Zurich, Switzerland, 2005

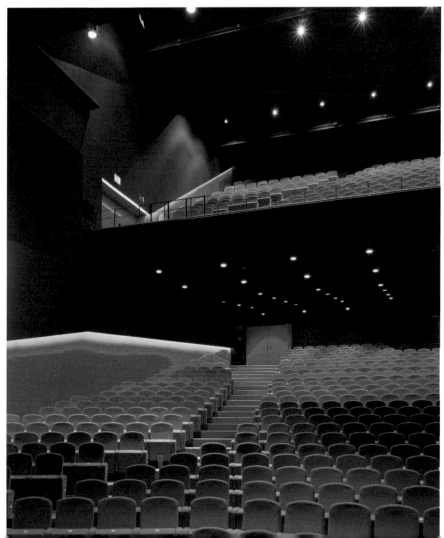

-145-

Abstract Plane

SHOGO ARATANI ARCHITECT & ASSOCIATES

www.ararchitect.com

TRAPEZOID
Hyogo, Japan, 2007

ATELIER BOW-WOW
www.bow-wow.jp

Sway House
Tokyo, Japan, 2008

For the Sway House, Yoshiharu Tsukamoto and Momoyo Kaijima of
Atelier Bow-Wow created a warped, twisted structure of tapering
proportions which will be used as living and working space by a
young, artistic couple.

This little house is built on a small site in Tokyo which was produced by dividing the old original lot into four parts and surrounding it with new mid-scale urban residences. They are very close to the house and block the sunlight. To ensure privacy and bright light inside, despite the surroundings, it is lit from the skylight which occupies half of the roof. At ground level the wall was twisted to afford parking space and became so-called HP (hyperbolic paraboloids). This wall, which is convex in the interior and concave in the exterior, gives a sense of internal and external reversal. It was emphasised by the light from the skylight which reflects off the convex surface and diffuses in the room. The children's room on the 3rd floor is in a tube-shaped box which is painted metallic orange to produce the reflective effect of light, colour and image. The ground surface is also shaped as HP and suggests the continuity and unity between the site and the house.

–148–

MASAHIRO IKEDA
with Akira Yoneda
www.roi-fund.com/masahiroikeda/

Delta
Tokyo, Japan, 2006

↳opposite page
HP
Tokyo, Japan, 2005

This small wooden house was designed for an elderly couple on a narrow and irregular-shape site in Tokyo. To maintain privacy the windows and openings are suppressed and outside views are shifted inside, or connect only to fragments of the outside through the crevices. The stainless exterior wall neutralises the peculiar outer shape with reflections on the surface and introduces outside images to the interior, as changing images. This house mediates between fragmentary city fabrics and different images, and finally structures them.

This four-level family home by Japanese architect Atelier Tekuto is shaped like a cut diamond or mineral and is half-buried in deep earth. Despite the small building site the architects succeeded in creating an overall feeling of spaciousness through the sharply defined concrete surfaces and angular windows. The distribution of living spaces does not follow any conventional order. The bedroom is in the basement, with the entrance and bathroom on the ground floor. The kitchen, living and dining rooms are located on the first floor while the bathroom is on the second floor. The building's polygonal shape also provided the opportunity for a covered parking space. A large rooflight was added to serve as a fire escape, to comply with building regulations.

Abstract Plane

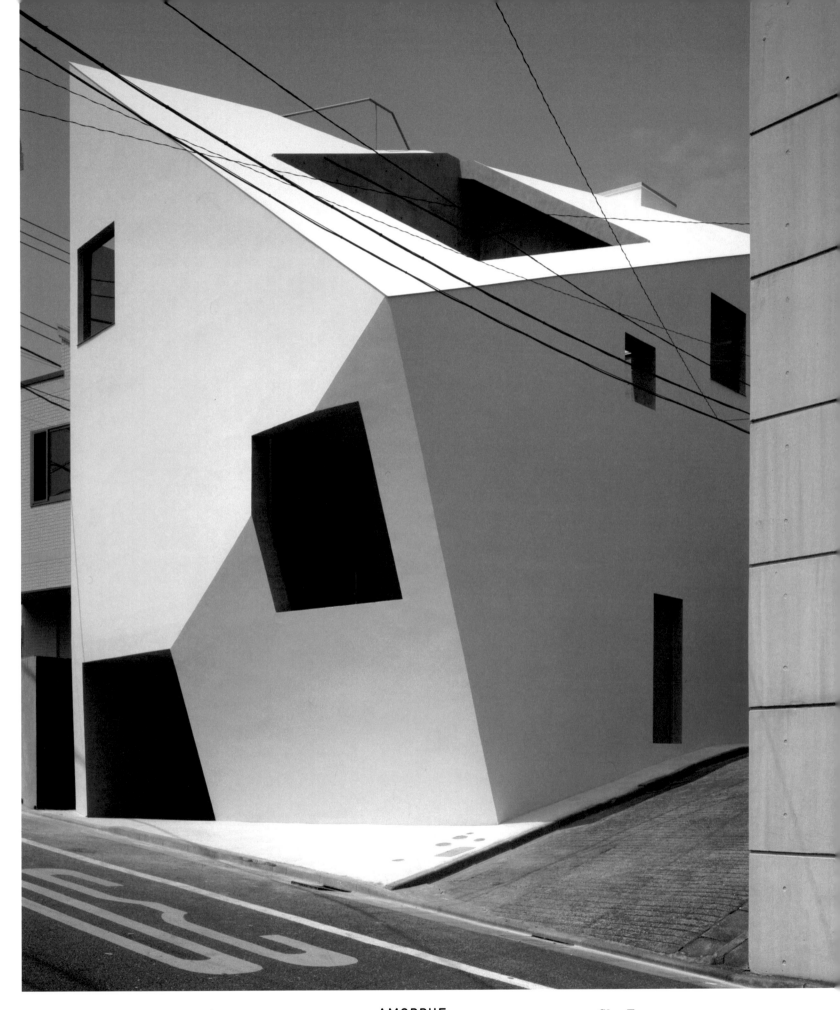

Abstract Plane

AMORPHE
Takeyama & Associates
www.amorphe.jp

Sky Trace
Tokyo, Japan, 2006

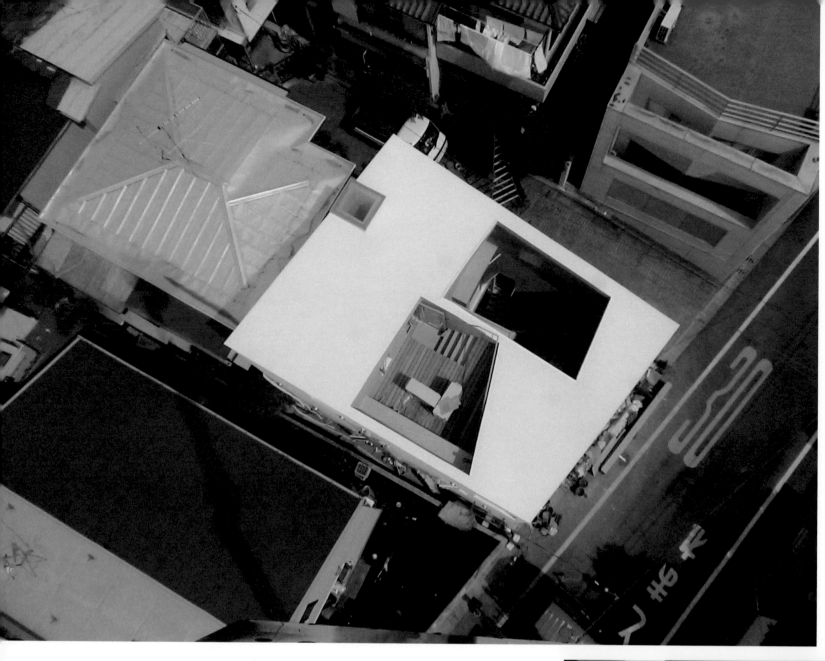

At the outset of the design, the occupants of the house, a family with two children, requested a spatial quality that would stimulate their creativity. Kiyoshi Sey Takeyama attempted to create a blank space in order to keep family members a good distance apart and to encourage their own lifestyles. The patio is an embodiment of this attempt. Passing through and penetrating this void, especially when looking up from the bottom of the patio, this blank space is symbolized by a fragment of the sky. So this patio is a trace of the sky, which acts both as a real and an ideal guiding element for the building

Abstract Plane

ATELIER BOW-WOW

www.bow-wow.jp

Mado Building
Tokyo, Japan, 2006

ISSHO ARCHITECTS
www.issho.com

Fudomae Apartment
Tokyo, Japan, 2006

Abstract Plane

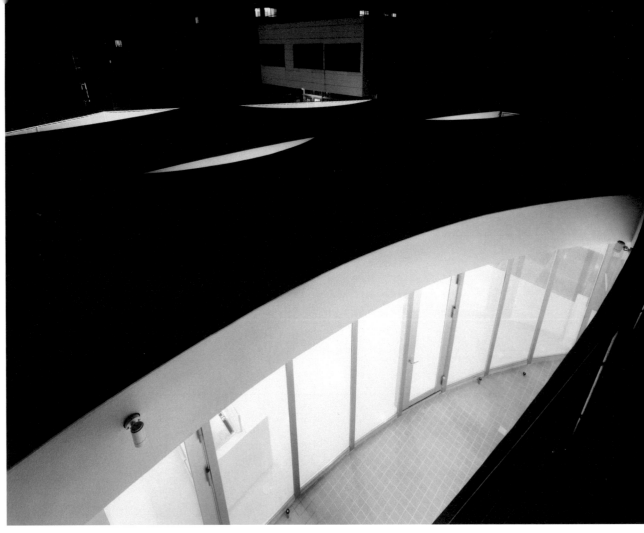

N MAEDA ATELIER
www5a.biglobe.ne.jp

Fontana
Numazu Shizuoka, Japan, 2005

The Fontana House by Norisada Maeda was inspired by the work
of Italian painter Lucio Fontana, who slashed blank canvases with
palette knives. The architects translated this practice into building
by replacing the 'canvas' with air. The originally homogenous volume of air on the site is slashed by 7 arched gardens.

Abstract Plane

KOCHI
www.kkas.net

Kn House
Kanagawa, Japan, 2006

MEIXNER SCHLÜTER WENDT
www.meixner-schlueter-wendt.de

Dornbusch Church
Frankfurt, Germany, 2004

The Dornbusch church is situated in a residential area in north Frankfurt. Due to
the poor condition of this 60 year old church and the extreme decline in attendance
at church services, complete demolition and building a new small "prayer room" as
a replacement were under discussion. Planning studies were able to show, however,
that the best choice was only partial demolition. From a town planning point of view,
a spatially and functionally intact ensemble remains – consisting of a community
centre, "residual church" and tower: a new churchyard, with an attractive potential
for public use, is created. The spacious area round the altar and the choir remains
as the old / new church. The open side of the building, created by the demolition
work, is closed with a new wall or façade. The special nature of this location and
the reduction process is made evident in that this new wall is marked with outlines
and moulds of the old church, i.e. the structures which have been removed - such as
the old entrance façade, altar and gallery now form a sculpted structure on the flat
wall surface. The outlines of the demolished church are painted on the churchyard
(asphalt) - a ground plan to stimulate pedestrians' imagination.

-162-

Abstract Plane

Abstract Plane

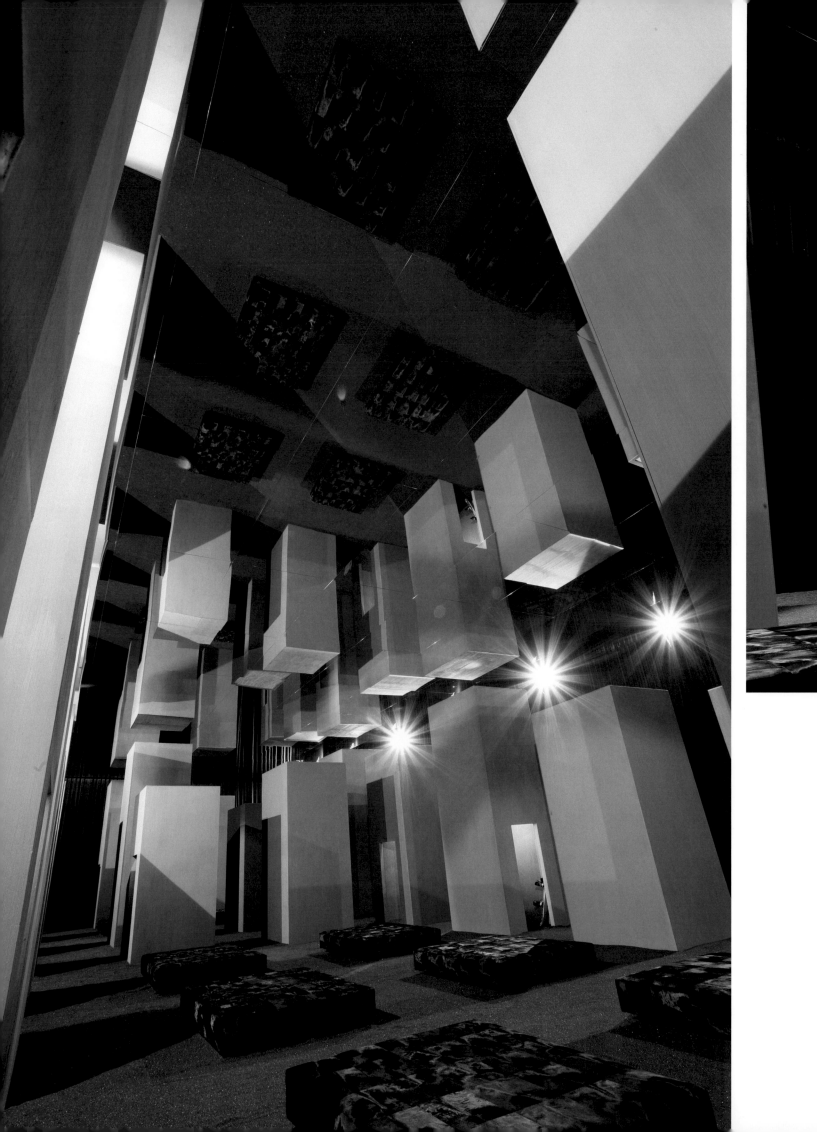

VILLA EUGÉNIE
www.villaeugenie.com

Hugo Boss – Firenze
Firenze, Italy, 2006

For the presentation of the new Hugo Boss collection at Pitti Uomo, Etienne Russo's Brussel-based Villa Eugénie, a company which designs and stages for and around the world of fashion, transformed a shed into a proper city of around 1000 square meter, with streets and avenues, skyscrapers and addresses, and the feeling of busy and buzzing city life. More than thirty cement-coated columns of different heights represented the megalopolis' skyscrapers, of which twelve were open to visitors to discover the Hugo Boss collections. The ceiling was fully covered with mirrors, creating a perspective of height, and a movie was projected from inside some of the columns on to back-projection screens, casting its images on the mirror ceiling for visitors to see: accelerated moving images of cars driving down the streets, stopping at traffic lights then moving again, images of people walking on the city streets, of street lights going on and off, were instrumental in reproducing the atmosphere of busy city life.

Abstract Plane

Abstract Plane

EMBAIXADA ARQUITECTURA
www.embaixada.net

Tomar Environmental Monitoring and Interpretation Offices (EMIO)
Tomar, Portugal, 2006

This project is a conversion of a former rundown infrastructure that plays a relevant role in the social and urban context of the city of Tomar. Located on the edge of the historic city centre, the building has been subjected to several attachments and changes over the years, finding itself threatened by some dilapidation, and inadequate for the intended use. The new programme comprises two distinct areas: a public area for exhibitions, meetings and cafeteria and a private area consisting of lecture rooms and accommodation for invited artists. To satisfy building regulations, the design maintains the entire external perimeter construction, while its rundown interior is totally removed. As a result of this and the functional programme, the new construction establishes itself as the anatomy of the existing building. The private areas are volumetrically defined within the structure, optimised for comfortable use, each with its own access, atmosphere, identity, shape, function and dimension.

COAST OFFICE
www.coastoffice.de

Villa Royal Roof
Odenwald, Germany, 2008

Odenwald with its scenic landscape is a well known and sought after destination amongst hikers and nature lovers. The site, a south-east slope, has a broad view over the countryside. Two volumes that are clearly defined in their colour, form and programme create differentiated interior spatial quality and varied relationships with the outside. The interplay of these spatial sculptures with staggering, shifting and overhangs reacts to the conditions of the place, the requirements of the family and the handling of building regulations.

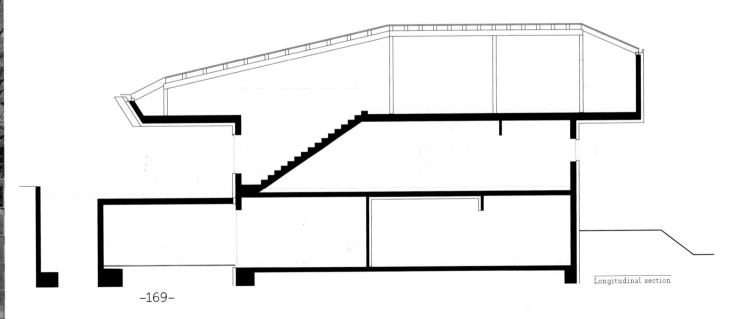

Longitudinal section

–169–

Abstract Plane

Abstract Plane

KIYONOBU NAKAGAME ARCHITECT & ASSOCIATES
www.nakagame.com

House in Futamatagawa
Yokohama, Japan, 2005

The house is located in an old residential district in the outskirts of Yokohama City. The architects were commissioned to design a house in the empty lot next to the client's already excisiting house.

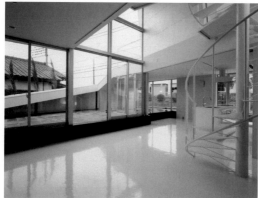

For this project the building's base develops into a seamless spiral plate that connects various functions of the house across all floors from ground level all the way to the roof. Six silver volumes that intersect the spiral form serve as structural pillars and at the same time define the spaces within the house.

N MADEA ATELIER
www5a.biglobe.ne.jp

Malibu
Utsunomiya Tochigi, Japan, 2006

01. Cross-section; 02. Longitudinal cross-section

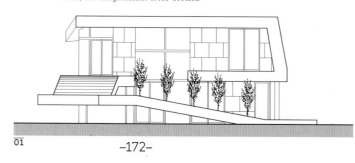

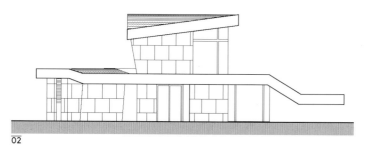

01

02

–172–

Abstract Plane

KIYONOBU NAKAGAME ARCHITECT & ASSOCIATES
www.nakagame.com

House in Izumi-Chuo
Yokohama, Japan, 2005

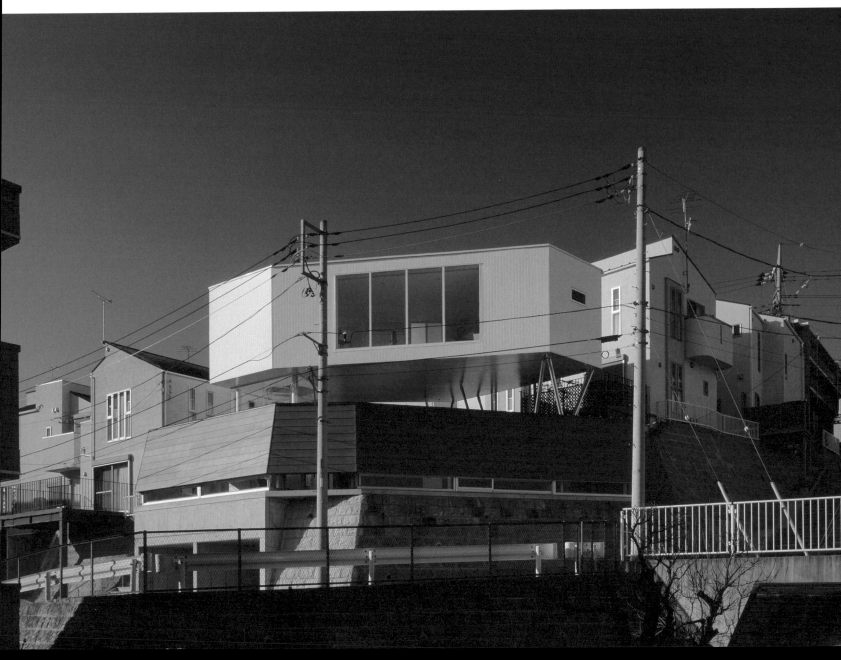

-174-

Abstract Plane

MASAHIRO IKEDA
www.roi-fund.com/masahiroikeda/

White Base
Toyko, Japan, 2006

This building is a home-come-studio for a young manga artist built
on a street packed with low-rise structures in suburban Tokyo. The
architecture was originally conceived as an index for an intermediate view linking distant and close views, in the light of the abrupt
urban disconnection and connection that occur every day in Tokyo.
The basement section including the dry area houses the studio.
Above ground is the parking space in a concrete box, and stacked
on top of it is the residential section made of sheet steel. An old
supercar is displayed in the parking space, as the artist's source of
creative imagination. It also serves as a pivotal point in a substitu-
tion which takes place above and below it, from the ground out to
the sky: a space of maximum volume is inserted underground, then
the mass of earth that had occupied this space is converted into a
unique object of steel, to be raised up in the air, defying gravity.

–175–

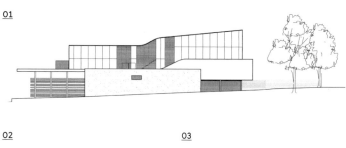

01

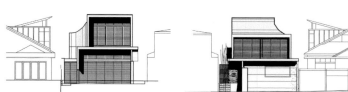

02 03

04

01. East elevation Floor; **02.** North elevation;
03. South elevaton; **04.** West elevation

KIYONOBU NAKAGAME ARCHITECT & ASSOCIATES

www.nakagame.com

House in Minami Boso
Chiba, Japan, 2007

TONY OWEN NDM
www.tondm.com.au

Bondi Wave house
Sydney, Australia, 2005

The design of this family house in Sydney's Bondi originated from a brief to marry the two dominant themes of this famous surf suburb – urban style and beach leisure – a combination that is not without precedent, if somewhat susceptible to cliché. Not so with Tony Owen's Wave House, which boasts a synthesis of considerably greater subtlety.

-177-

ÁLVARO SIZA

Ibere Camargo Foundation
Porto Alegre, Brazil, 2008

Abstract Plane

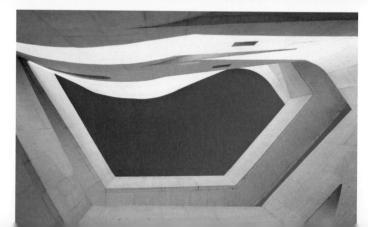

The state-of-the-art exhibition space and cultural centre designed by Portuguese architect Álvaro Siza is a big rectangular white structure, curved outlines of which were implemented by the use of reinforced concrete. The building houses the collection of over four thousand works by the master of Brazilian Expressionism, and is intended to be a major centre for discussion, research and exhibitions of modern and contemporary art. The project model has already won the Venice Biennial of Architecture's Gold Lion award in 2002.

Abstract Plane

LYONS
www.lyonsarch.com.au

Hume City Council
Broadmeadows, Australia, 2007

MRDV
www.mvrdv.nl

Gyre
Tokyo, Japan, 2007

The programme of this luxurious shopping centre in Tokyo indicates a building that can serve one or several users/companies. It communicates on two scale levels: the level of the building as a whole and the level of the individual shops inside the building. The space is programmed for seven floors, each floor area is 60 per cent of the total plot. By gradually twisting these floors around a central core, a series of terraces emerge, connected by stairs and elevators positioned outside the volumes. They create an identical pair of vertically-stepped, terraced streets, one on each side of the core. The exterior of the building produces a highly iconic and sculptural form; a building that attracts and invites people, not only on to the street level, but also to companies and destinations at higher levels.

As the Tetris game-inspired building by Ofis Arhitekti in Ljubljana faces a busy highway, the apartment entrances and balconies are shifted towards the quieter south-facing side, as 30-degree window-wings. For the future, two further blocks are planned on both longitudinal sides, so no windows will face directly east and west. Each apartment looks towards its own balcony, and in some cases there is also a glazed loggia.

TRUE COLORS

"DON'T BE AFRAID TO LET THEM SHOW YOUR TRUE COLORS. **TRUE COLORS** ARE BEAUTIFUL LIKE A RAINBOW." Cyndi Lauper

True Colors is about architectural feasts for the eye that don't shy away from ardently committing themselves to the full spectrum of colours. The projects presented in this chapter include amongst others a number of impressive interiors, daring event designs, renovations of existing buildings from the inside out, light-façades and large-scale projects such as entire housing complexes.

AB ROGERS DESIGN
with Shona Kitchen and Dominic Robson (BLINK!.)

www.abrogers.com

Gomme des Garçons
Paris, France, 2001

The Comme des Garcons flagship store won the "International Interior Design Award 2001" in the category Best Store Design, and its interior is composed of smooth, reflective Ferrari red fibreglass.

True Colors

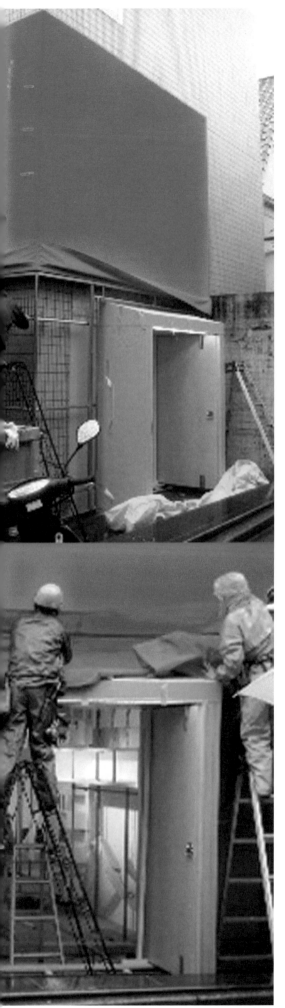

FRANKLIN AZZI ARCHITECTURE

www.franklinazzi.com

Red Military Tent

Tokyo, Japan, 2004

The military Red Tent project gives us another radical image based on the archetype of military tents. The textile is initially beige or kaki then, in a very arbitrary manner, like the intervention of an artist, the fabric is suddenly turned red, it is transvestied, touched to the very heart of the fibres. The main idea is to impose an archetype out of its initial geographical context onto the street and city space. By playing on the common imagination, the object of fiction is thus revealed by the geographical move of a strong architectural archetype. Once away from its initial space, the object reflects a sideways image that moves the surrounding urban space.

The project is made of a façade of red oiled fabric, held by natural leather straps and suspended by a metallic structure. This fabric is held at the bottom by sandbags. The entrance is through a metallic chamber.

AB ROGERS DESIGN
with Wolff Olins, Sara Fanelli, Illuminations, Spiral, Praline and Dominic Robson (BLINK!.)
www.abrogers.com

Tate Modern: Redevelopment of Level 3 and 5 Concourses
London, United Kingdom, 2006

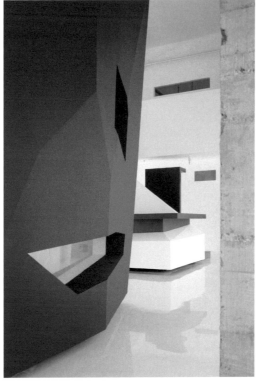

The faceted red object is part of the conversion of a former factory in the centre of Shanghai by Italian architect Francesco Gatti. It contains two meeting rooms and a kitchen on its lower level. It is separated from the floor by an illuminated slice of void and it reflects onto the white resin. Other less startling sculptures are the reception desk which is placed in the bend of the banister on the stairs and another long belt-like area which can be used as a working surface and which leads the way into the central area.

3GATTI
www.3gatti.com

Red object
Shanghai, China, 2006

ROJKIND ARQUITECTOS
www.rojkindarquitectos.com

Nestlé Museum of Chocolate
Toluca, Mexico, 2007

The entire horizontal sculptural structure of Mexican architect
Michel Rojkind's Chocolate Museum, situated on the main highway
into Paseo Tollocan, has become an instant landmark for tourists
arriving to tour the Nestle factory. The multi-faceted structure creates compelling abstract spaces inside with its twists and turns;
it houses a child-friendly visitor's reception area, a museum shop,
and a theatre. From the outside, the museum recalls folding origami
shapes with its subtly zigzagging volumes.

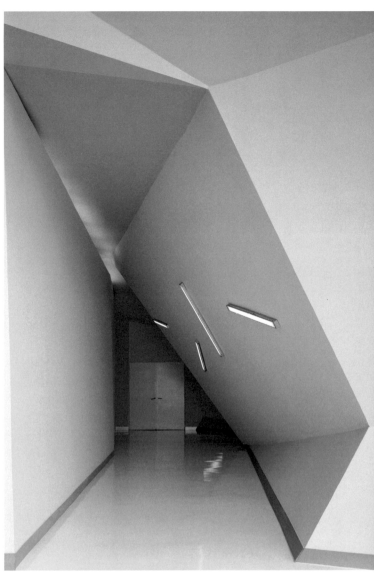

ASYMPTOTE
Hani Rashid and Lise Anne Couture
www.asymptote.net

Allesi Flagship Store
New York, USA, 2006

–197–

<u>True Colors</u>

FAK3
Johnny Wong
www.fak3.com

Miele Boutique
Hong Kong, China, 2006

This project by FAK3, founded by Johnny Wong, is a renovation of a boutique showroom in Causeway Bay, Hong Kong. The curtain wall façade of the slick store front is in red to black reflective graduated glass, hand crafted in Guangzhou, China. The boutique sits like a mist-filled, crystal prism off Hysan Avenue, an exclusive fashion-focused shopping area, rubbing shoulders with the likes of Louis Vuitton, Hermes and the Chanels.

BERNARD KHOURY / DW5
www.bernardkhoury.com

B018
Beirut, Libanon, 1998

B018 is a music club, a nocturnal refuge at the "Quarantaine", a site that was better known for its macabre aura. The "Quarantaine" is located near the port of Beirut. During the French protectorate, it was a place of quarantine for arriving crews. In the recent war it became home to Palestinian, Kurdish and South Lebanese refugees (20,000 in 1975). In January 1976, local militiamen launched a radical attack that completely wiped out the area. The slums were demolished along with the kilometre-long boundary wall that isolated the zone from the city. Over twenty years later, the scars of war are still perceptible through the disparity between the scarce urban fabric of the area and the densely populated neighborhoods located across the highway that borders the zone. The B018 project is, first of all, a reaction to difficult and explosive conditions that are inherent to the history of its location and the contradictions that are implied by the implementation of an entertainment programme on such a site. B018 refuses to connive with the naive amnesia that governs post-war reconstruction efforts. The project is built below ground. Its façade is pressed into the ground to avoid over-exposure for a mass that could act as a rhetorical monument. The building is embedded in a circular concrete disc slightly above tarmac level. In repose, it is almost invisible. It comes to life in the late hours of the night when its articulated roof structure constructed in heavy metal retracts hydraulically. The opening of the roof exposes the club to the world above and reveals the cityscape as an urban backdrop to the patrons below.

-200-

True Colors

True Colors

ROBERTNEUN™
www.robertneun.com

Bar Tausend
Berlin, Germany, 2007

BINC INTERIORSTUFF
Eric Kuster

www.binc.nl

ARC
Amsterdam, the netherlands, 2001

↳opposite page
STAAT AMSTERDAM

www.staatamsterdam.nl

House of Bols
Amsterdam, The Netherlands, 2007

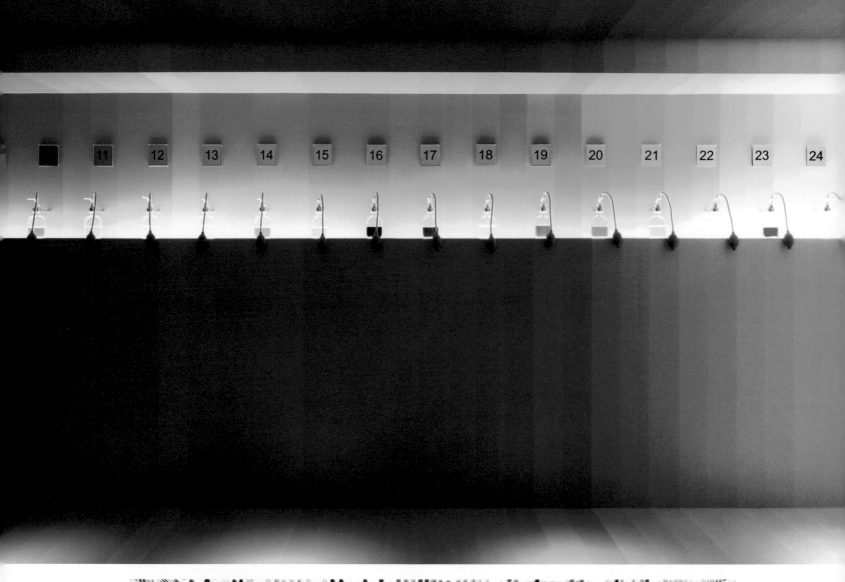

True Colors

METRO ARQUITETURA
with Juliano Dubeux
www.metro.arq.br

Club Nox
Refice, Brazil, 2005

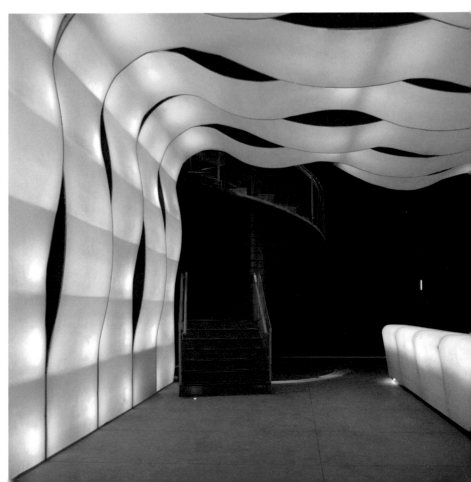

-208-

ANDY TONG CREATIONS
www.andycreations.com

WTCmore Demo Parlour
Hong Kong, China, 2006

To promote the transformation of the Hong Kong World Trade Centre, a show suite – the WTCmore Demo Parlour - has been created using the cross-over concept to demonstrate a new retail experience, mixing and matching shopping and leisure activities.

WONDERWALL INC.

www.wonder-wall.com

Bape Store
Tokyo, Japan, 2007

PÉRIPHÉRIQUES ARCHITECTES

www.peripheriques-architectes.com

Kaleidoscopic Garden
Nagoya, Japan, 2007

VILLA EUGÉNIE
www.villaeugenie.com

Boss Orange Collection
Plaza de Torros, Barcelona, Spain, 2007

For the Boss Orange spring/summer collection, Villa Eugénie created a show, fitting the collection inspired by the science-fiction movie Blade Runner, into a bullfighting arena that was transformed into a spaceship. A circular catwalk surrounded the arena where the audience was seated, facing the spectators' stands, which were left empty. A battery-powered LED light was placed on each of the 80,000 seats of the empty spectators' stands, providing light for about six hours. Above the LEDS, projected images of spaceships and astronauts hovered in all directions. A black hole effect was created in the sky by directing beams of light from above.

STUDIO 63
www.studio63.it

Novo Department Store
Hong Kong, China, 2007

-216-

SERIE LONDON
Chris Lee with Kapil Gupta
www.serie.co.uk

Blue Frog Acoustic Lounge and Studios
Mumbai, India, 2007

A large north-lit industrial warehouse within the old mill district in Mumbai is to be converted into a complex of sound recording studios and an acoustic lounge. This lounge consists of a restaurant, bar and a live stage. Beyond this amalgamation of provisions, Blue Frog seeks to stage an acoustic experience par excellence. The undulating height of the seating booths is gently modulated by a glowing acrylic resin surface, which unifies the disparate types and asserts the presence of the architecture, even in the midst of the spectacle of a state-of-the-art sound and light show at the Blue Frog.

ELECTRIC DREAMS
www.electricdreams.se

Weekday Malmö
Malmö, Sweden, 2006

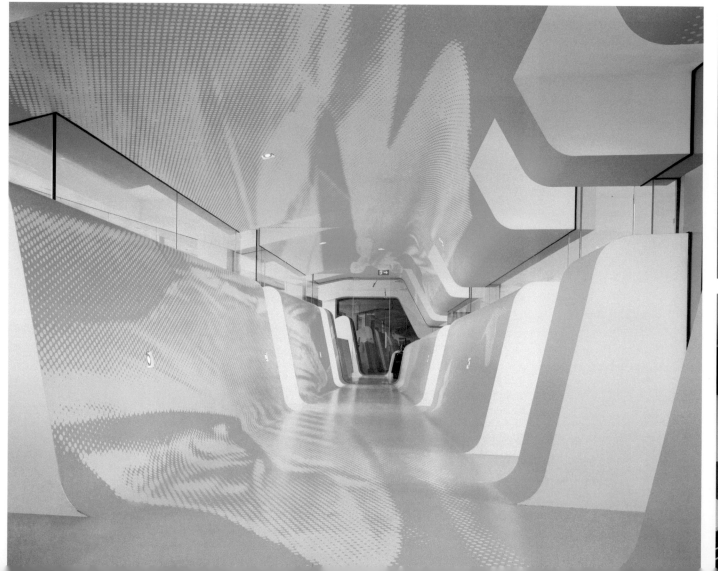
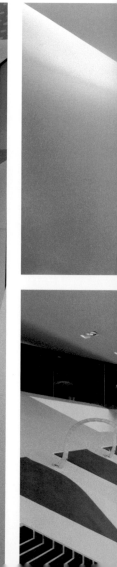

GRAFT
www.graftlab.com

KU64
Berlin, Germany, 2005

Few environments are as negatively freighted in terms of expectation as a dental clinic. A hygienic and sterile atmosphere, the classical "white colour range" and last but not least the typical smell are very much connected with a feeling of a physical and psychological state of emergency and even abuse. Against this background, Graft architects created a radically new typology for the Dr. Ziegler's Dental Clinic. The model of a dune landscape with high points and hollows to hide in was used as a metaphor for an artificial landscape of undulating folded floors reflected by a ceiling of a similar shape. This creates a space that provides a lush definition of introverted protection without distinct enclosure. Anamorphotic images in white are screen printed onto the general orange surface and can only be deciphered from distinct viewpoints. The space continuously changes as you walk through it. Furniture, as well as functions such as storage and technical equipment, has been invisibly integrated into the sculpture of the space.

GIORGIO BORRUSO DESIGN
www.borrusodesign.com

Fornarina Flagship Store
London, United Kingdom, 2006

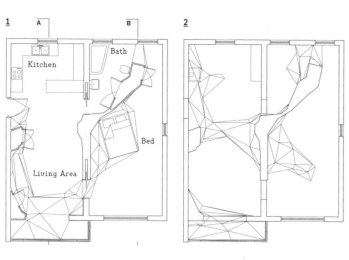

1

2

3

4

01.+ 02. Floor plans
03. Longitudinal section
04. Cross-section

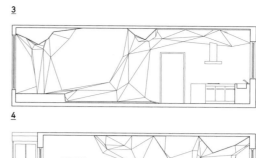

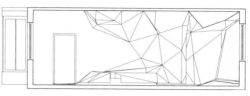

SCISKEW COLLABORATIVE
www.scisckew.com

Fumin Road Apartment
Shanghai, China, 2005

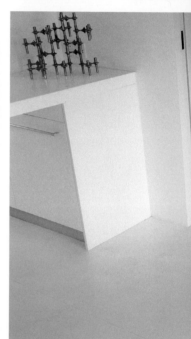

-222-

True Colors

True Colors

QUEESTE
www.queestearchitecten.nl

Maff Apartment
The Hague, The Netherlands, 2007

Maff Apartment is a hotel room located on the third floor in the attic of a private house in The Hague. The client and owner lives in the same building. A communal staircase provides access to the apartment, which functions autonomously from the rest of the building. The aim of the design was to create a living environment that would be spacious despite the small volume, providing all the comforts expected from luxurious contemporary accommodation. In addition, Maff Apartment was to have a clear and strong identity to provide a sense of uniqueness for its users.

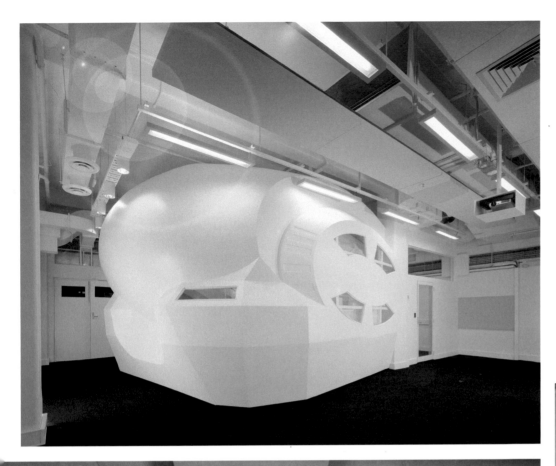

PAUL MORGAN ARCHITECTS
www.paulmorganarchitects.com

SIAL Sound Studios
RMIT University, Melbourne, Australia, 2005

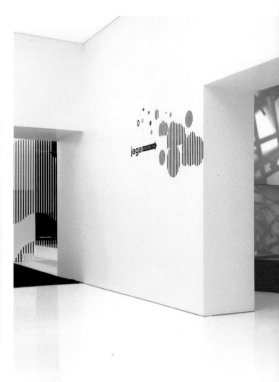

STUDIO ARNE QUINZE
www.studioarnequinze.tv

Jaga Experience Lab
Diepenbeek, Belgium, 2006

A showroom turned into an experience lab that shows no products but creates an atmosphere inspired by a lung. The room has a fully installed sound system, 10 projection screens and allows the visitor to become inspired by fire and heat through all senses.

-227-

Zuri Bar
Knokke, Belgium, 2007

N MAEDA ATELIER
www5a.biglobe.ne.jp/~norisada

Inax / Ginza Showroom
Tokyo, Japan, 2007

Norisada Maeda created an impressive interior for this tile manufacturer's showroom, pasting a vast number of white and red mosaic tiles on an curved concrete surface.

AB ROGERS DESIGN
with D.A. Studio and Dominic Robson (BLINK!.)
www.abrogers.com

Emperor Moth
London, United Kingdom, 2006

Emperor Moth is a new and dynamic Russian fashion label designed by Katia Gomi-
ashvili, who commissioned Ab Rogers to create a new store in Mayfair, London
including all the branding and packaging. Inspired by Nikki de Saint Phalle's Tarot
Garden and Robert Smithson's mirrors, Ab Rogers Design created a voluptuous internal space. Mirrors have always fascinated, from the Russian Constructivists to the
Fabergé eggs. Mirrors suggest preciousness, dynamism, modernity and nostalgia.
They are central to the concept of the new Emperor Moth store.

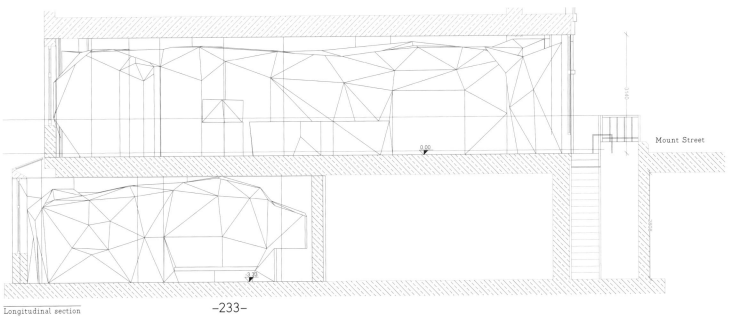

Mount Street

Longitudinal section

True Colors

KARIM RASHID
www.karimrashid.com

Majik Café
Belgrade, Serbia, 2008

KARIM RASHID
www.karimrashid.com

Casa Digitalia
Milan, Italy, 2008

KARIM RASHID
www.karimrashid.com

Bosco Pi Shopping Mall
Moscow, Russia, 2008

GRAFT
www.graftlab.com

Lofts for Zeal Pictures Europe
Berlin, Germany, 2003

The entrance into a new complex of lofts in a former factory building at near the river Spree in Berlin is formed by an old freight elevator, which was due to be demolished. GRAFT re-used and reshaped the elevator as a vertical multi-media vestibule, creating an individual entry scenario for each loft by storyboarding the experience of the client to the offices.

BAUPILOTEN
www.baupiloten.com

Erika Mann Elementary School
Berlin, Germany, 2003

The Baupiloten are a group of students at the architectural faculty of the Technical University Berlin who carry out building projects under the guidance and supervision of architect Susanne Hofmann. Working with the pupils, Baupiloten developed and created the imaginary landscape of the Silver Dragon to form a basis for expressive and playful architecture: the further you get into the school building, the more strongly you feel the spirit of the Silver Dragon - a spirit which alters, resonates, glows and shimmers. Sensuous architecture, socially engaged and experimental.

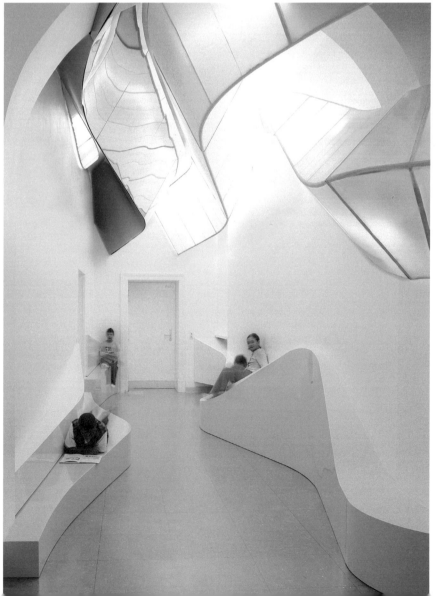

ATELIER HITOSHI ABE
www.a-slash.jp

Space of Rainbow
Shiogama, Japan, 2006

–240–

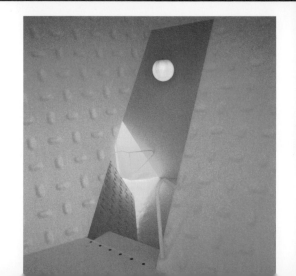

True Colors

JÜRGEN MAYER H.
www.jmayerh.com

Housewarming MyHome
Weil am Rhein, Germany, 2007

Housewarming MyHome is part of a larger group
show at the Vitra Design Museum. The exhibition
focuses on contemporary questions concerning
the affects of living with and amongst a collection of various installation works. Housewarming
MyHome extends the Museum Café into the exhibition area with a large supergraphic displayed
on the floor, walls and ceiling, thus blurring their
spatial boundaries. Certain zones of the wall and
seating surfaces are covered with a heat-sensitive
coating which turns white when warmed. Built
in hot wires are programmed to turn on and off,
creating temporary ornamental clusters of parallel
white lines, which unexpectedly appear and dis-
appear in rhythm as they warm up and cool down.

UN STUDIO
Ben van Berkel and Caroline Bos
www.unstudio.com

Holiday Home
Institute of Contemporary Art, Philadelphia, USA, 2006

The Holiday Home is an experiential installation exploring and quantifying areas in which the holiday home departs from modern design conventions. The orthogonal surfaces of the archetypal house are extruded and skewed, creating the sculptural envelope within which the dichotomies of home and holiday home are played out. The new architectural shape emulates escapism, the expectation of a holiday as removed from the everyday experiential routine. The interplay of what is real and what is virtual transpires on a number of levels, touching on ideas of collective memory and phenomenological perceptions.

–244–

COAST OFFICE
www.coastoffice.de

HUGS / Herzog-Ulrich Elementary School
Lauffen am Neckar, Germany, 2008

The Herzog Ulrich Elementary School building dates from 1907 and underwent a striking refurbishment by Coast Office. Clearly defined "space furniture" identifies rooms and areas and forms a contrast with the existing landmark building at the same time. Strongly coloured spaces create identity and make a stay into an experience. The colour intensity of the rooms corresponds to the intensity of their use. Each school day begins and ends by passing up or down the new staircase. The pink-coloured space is a kind of colour gate into the school world.

ZANDERROTH ARCHITEKTEN
www.zanderroth.de

Elementary School Schulzendorf
Schulzendorf, Germany, 2007

True Colors

5+1AA
www.5piu1aa.com

Edificio Stecca
Milan, Italy, 2006

A new area is coming to life in Milan: the area of
Porta Vittoria, together with its new empty spaces to fill in and its contradictions to interpret,
handle, emphasise. Within this area, the complex
of Frigoriferi Milanesi-Palazzo del Ghiaccio has
a predominant role. It is composed of a short and
long building, located along Via Piranesi. It is a
banal and dull building, but it plays a key role
from the perspective point of view with respect
to other important buildings beyond the line. The
lack of personality of the long and low building
will be highlighted by two simple processes: on
the one hand a coat of black paint will replace the
grey colour, a blob which assails everything: walls,
windows, profiles, in order to obliterate any form
of architectonic ratiocination and to transform
the structure into a black hole, swallowing everything; on the other a new shiny "skin-peel", made
of glass, will be overlapped in order to create a
chromatic effect with respect to the monotone
geometry of the surrounding area; it unedges the
volume with a bidimensional and "night" effect.

-249-

Airspace Tokyo is a design effort synthesizing the work of two architecture practices: Hajime Masubuchi Studio M and Thom Faulders/Thom Faulders Architecture with Sean Ahlquist / Proces2. They worked independently from two different cities: Hajime Masubuchi in Tokyo contributed the design for the building, and Thom Faulders, with Proces2 in San Francisco, created the design for the exterior screen façade.

Approaching the project from diverse points of view and with different design sensibilities, they kept up an ongoing dialogue, with an eye to the layering of the final combined architectural outcome.

Though created through different design methodologies, Airspace Tokyo is not ultimately conceived as a separation of the proportionally orthogonal building and its amorphous screen façade, but rather as an architectural synthesis and programmatic integration. The expansive living environments and irregular cellular voids infiltrate and leak into each other visually, creating a living airspace packed with possibility.

STUDIO M
with Thom Faulders Architecture and PROCES2
www.s-t-m.jp; www.beigedesign.com; www.process2.com

Airspace Tokyo
Tokyo, Japan, 2007

BRISAC-GONZALES
www.brisacgonzales.com

Multi Purpose Hall
Aurillac, France, 2007

This building by Cécile Brisac and Edgar Gonzalez is a new venue for theatre, concerts, fairs and sports events in Aurrilac, situated at the edge of France's Massif Central mountain region. As it is never permanently inhabited, the building is essentially a chamber for ephemeral events. Three ribbons of concrete that vary in height and texture define the building. The ribbons delineate the different zones of the building: entry, hall, storage and back of house facilities. Externally the upper ribbon is made of prefabricated concrete panels with a regular grid of glass bricks. During the day, the sunlight plays with the 25,000 bespoke pyramidal-shaped glass bricks, producing glimmering effects and dramatic shadows. In the evening the building awakens as the surfaces of the glass bricks, like Fresnel lenses, amplify the intensity of the coloured lighting scheme, producing a glittering façade. The façade's colour lighting scheme can be altered to match the event inside.

MASS STUDIES
www.massstudies.com

Xi Gallery
Pusan, Korea, 2007

Located in Yeonsan-dong, Pusan, this four-storey building was constructed to promote "Xi," a brand of apartments. In addition to the standard type of apartment unit
exhibition space (a common practice in Korea for publicising and marketing prospec-
tive buildings), an even larger share of the floor area is allocated as a variable cultural space for the locals, thus creating a brand new building typology: a Housing and
Cultural Centre which subsequently opens up possibilities for progressive culture.

True Colors

MASS STUDIES
www.massstudies.com

Oktokki Space Center
Incheon, Korea, 2007

True Colors

The Oktokki Space Centre is a theme park situated on a sloping site on Ganghwa Island. The centre comprises educational exhibits and indoor/outdoor interactive facilities for children, focusing on space science and space aeronautics. The hall contains exhibition space and visitor lounges over four storeys of varying heights. A wide range of exhibition and audiovisual facilities can be arranged freely, with diverse interconnections at all levels. The majority of the building is absorbed by the sloping topography, its exposure minimised, while the building's upper section extends into the surrounding landscape to create a new and different topography. At the same time, the variety of levels and movement paths inside the building expand outdoors to blend in with the entire site's pedestrian continuity/circulation network.

PÉRIPHÉRIQUES ARCHITECTS
www.peripheriques-architectes.com

Atrium, Jussieu University
Paris, France, 2006

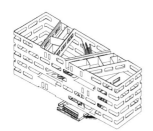

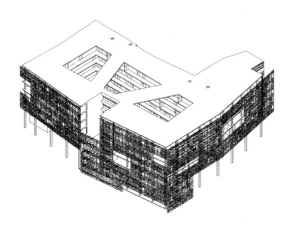

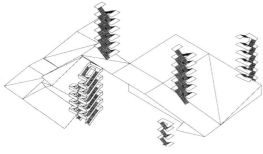

01. Conceptual diagram

At ground floor level of the Jussieu University Building by
Périphériques Architects, the existing slab on which the university
buildings are built folds up in an origami-like ramp to even up the
natural and built levels in a fluid movement. The glass and metal
skin composed of ten types of panel perforated with circular holes
of different sizes gives the façades complex and variable depth. The
holes also filter daylight and reflections over the glass surface, creating shimmering effects that give the building a constantly changing look, reminding us that the original plan has altered.

This rooftop house extension positions the bedrooms as separate houses on top of an existing monumental house and atelier, optimising the privacy of every member of the family. The houses are distributed in such a way that a series of plazas, streets and alleys seem like a mini-village on top of the building. Parapet walls with windows surround the new village. Trees, tables, open-air showers and benches are added, optimising the rooftop life. Finishing all elements with a blue polyurethane coating creates a new "heaven", a crown on top of the monument. The addition can be seen as a prototype for a further condensation of the old and existing city.

CHRIS BOSSE
www.chrisbosse.de

Watercube
Beijing, China, 2008

MVRDV
www.mvrdv.nl

Didden Village
Rotterdam, The Netherlands, 2007

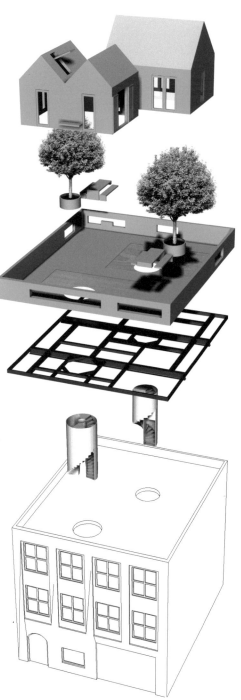

EDUARDO LONGO
www.eduardolongo.com

Casa Bola
São Paulo, Brazil, since 1979

ARCHITECTURAL BODY RESEARCH FOUNDATION
Arakawa + Madeline Gins
www.reversibledestingy.org

Reversible Destiny Lofts (In Memory of Helen Keller)
Mitaka, Japan, 2007

Since 1963, artists-architects-poets Arakawa and
Madeline Gins have worked togteher to produce
visionary, boundary-defying art and architecture,
and have founded the Architectural Body Research
Foundation. »

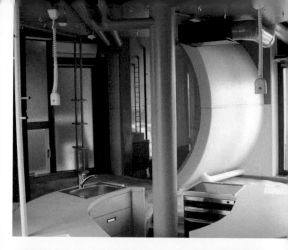

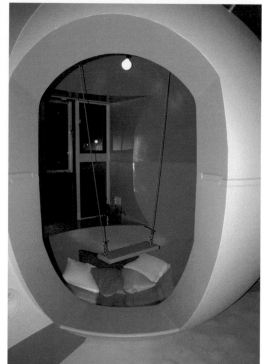

"Not only does a resident of a Mitaka reversible destiny loft live as an architectural body, she also lives as a biotopologist. She becomes an architectural body by fully associating herself with her surroundings. She lives and works as a biotopologist by taking cognizance of and tracking far more action ranges than are usually taken account of."

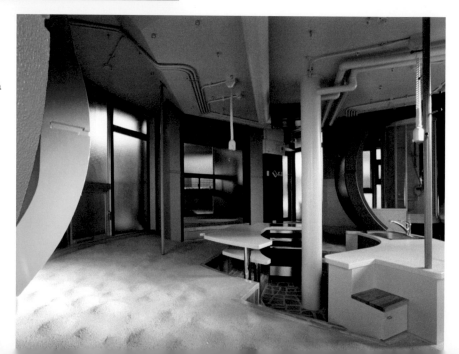

ARCHITECTURAL BODY RESEARCH FOUNDATION
Arakawa + Madeline Gins
www.reversibledestingy.org

Bioscleave House
East Hampton, USA, 2008

Start by thinking of architecture as tentatively constructing
towards a holding in place. Architecture's holding in place occurs
within and as part of a prevailing atmospheric condition that others routinely call biosphere but which architects, feeling the need
to stress its dynamic nature, have renamed bioscleave. The Bioscleave House operates as an inter-active laboratory of everyday life.
This fully symmetrical house, with a sloping sculpted floor and
walls that connect in unexpected ways, will map perception and
diagrammatically display the set of tendencies and coordinating
skills fundamental to human capability.

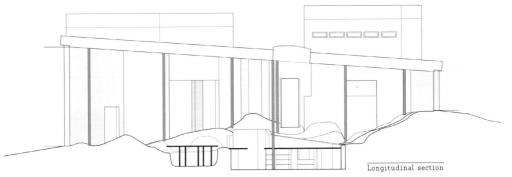

Longitudinal section

True Colors

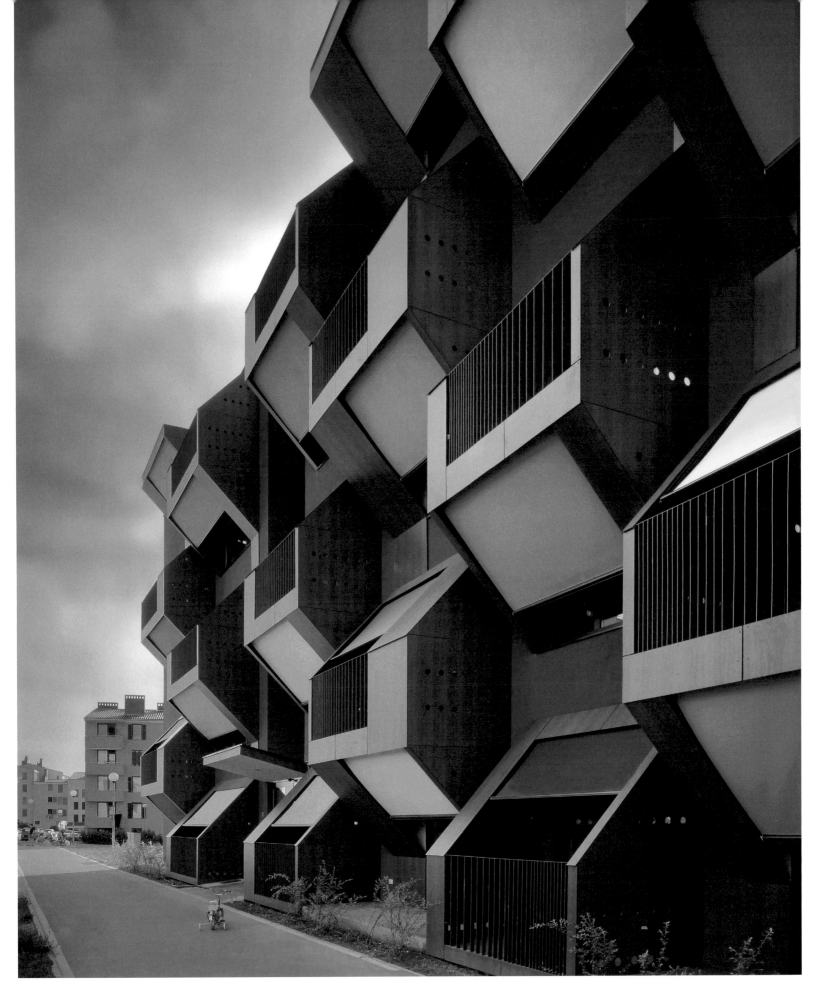

OFIS ARHITEKTI
www.ofis-a.si

Social Housing
Izola, Slovenia, 2006

This project is a winning entry for two housing blocks in a competition organised by the Slovenia Housing Fund, a government-run programme providing low-cost apartments for young families. The proposal won on economic, rational and functional grounds, but mostly for the ratio between gross versus saleable surface area and the flexibility of the plans. The blocks are set out on a hill with a view of Izola Bay on one side and of the surrounding hills on the other. The brief stipulated 30 apartments of different sizes and structures, varying from studio flats to three-bedroom apartments. The apartments are not large, with very small rooms by Slovenian standards. There are no structural elements inside the apartments, thus providing flexibility and the chance to reorganise things. The building's strong colours create different atmospheres within the apartments.

Various floor plans

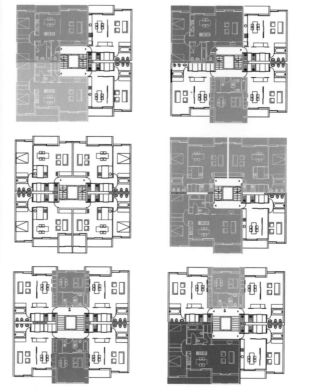
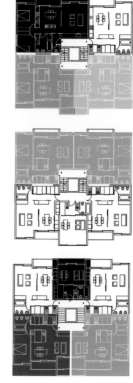

True Colors

The refurbishment of the old Santa Caterina Market, located in the old city of Barcelona, is a development of the whole urban texture, "blending and mixing" with the original building, and thus creating a new canopy reminiscent of the primitive one. The curved canopy is achieved with a laminated wood structure, which rests on big tubular lattice girders, resting on a series of concrete portals: the original archways with the more classic trusses were retained on the sides of the building.

-273-

True Colors

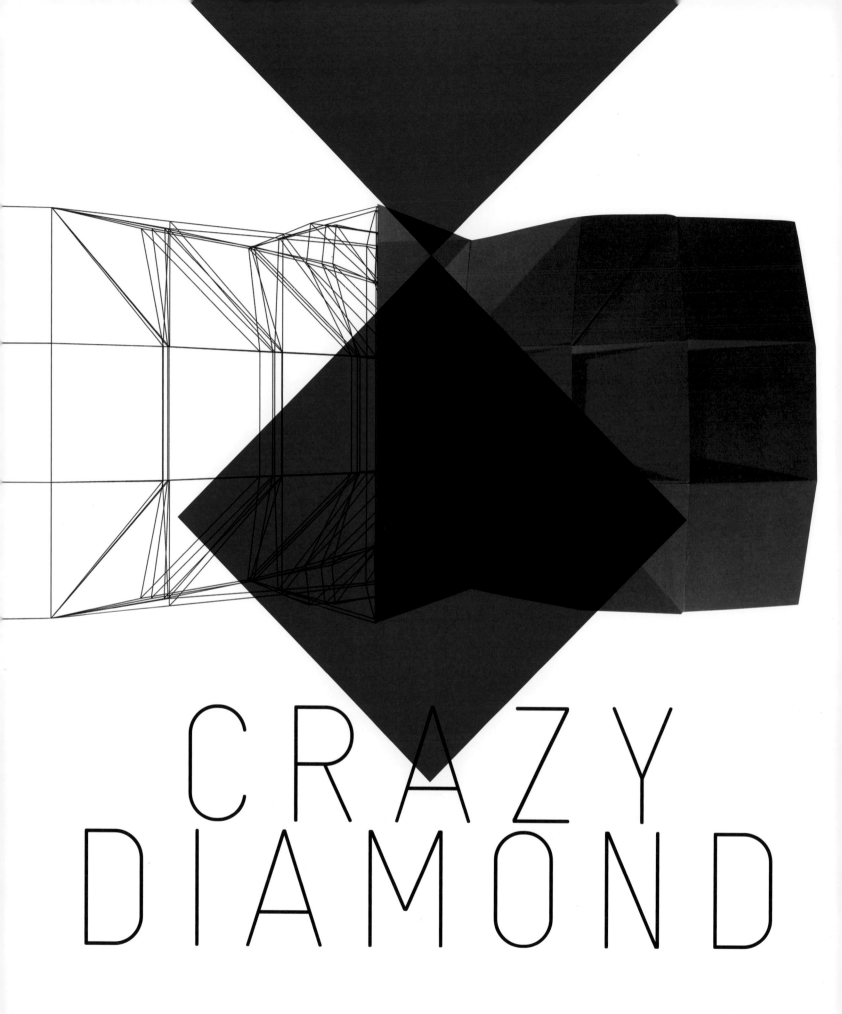

CRAZY
DIAMOND

"THREATENED BY SHADOWS AT NIGHT AND EXPOSED IN THE LIGHT, SHINE ON YOU CRAZY DIAMOND." Pink Floyd

The concluding chapter, Crazy Diamond, traces a wide variety of projects that seem to seek inspiration from crystalline forms and lucid structures. Here projects are aligned that encompass everything from small-scale interior designs to high-rises, for which only the sky seems to be the limit. The kaleidoscopic spectrum of styles inherent in these works reflects the elemental force and creative wealth of contemporary architecture practices.

BAUPILOTEN
www.baupiloten.com

Kindergarten "Tree of Dreams"
Berlin, Germany, 2005

Following the take-over by the institution known as the Arbeiter-Samariter-Bund, the day-care centre received its new name and a new resident: the Tree of Dreams. The Tree of Dreams quickly settled down with the children and is now their companion and playmate. His Trunk World sprawls along the ground floor. It is impressive and massive. The trunk encloses you from all sides and gives you the feeling of security. The Dream Blossoms grow out of the trunk and the children can snuggle themselves into them. Above the blossoms grows the Leaves' World. The mirrored silver leaves magically reflect rays of sunlight into the darker Trunk World.

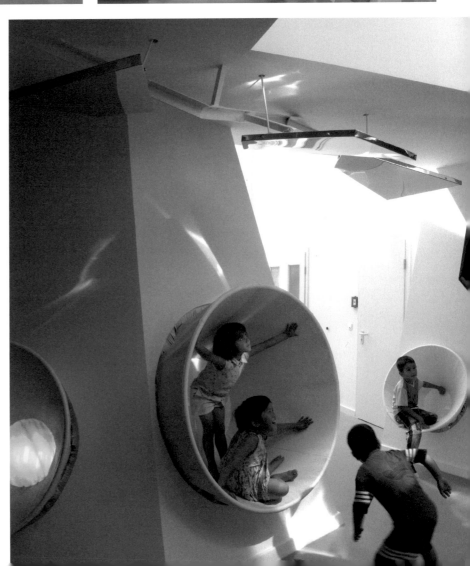

Abstract Plane

Crazy Diamond

SERERO ARCHITECTS
with ITERAE Architecture

Acoustical Domes
Rome, Italy, 2005

David Serero's work investigates new architectural forms for theatres. His research based on the manipulation of acoustical, topographical, and light fields develops parametric forms that create a basis for inventing of new forms of theatres in which space itself maintains an open and flexible relationship with the artwork, the spectator and its environment. His variable geometry Acoustical Domes emerge from research on the computation of acoustics and the propagation and reflection of sound in space. Sound, which is both a physical and immaterial phenomenon, is used here as the context for a spatial intervention in a 40 feet high Renaissance Salon at Villa Medici with a terrible echo. A surface was deployed in space with a geometry that allows for its transformation in time and the modification of the acoustical behaviour of the space. This device makes it possible to adjust the volume of the room and hence its reverberation time. This "Dome", like the architectural archetype, permits interaction between the volume of the room and the propagation of music.

NIKKEN SEKKEI
Tomohiko Yamanashi and Tatsuya Hatori
www.nikken.co.jp/

Jimbocho Theater Building
Tokyo, Japan, 2007

This landmark building was designed by the studio of Tomohiko Yamanashi and Tasuya Hatori of Nikken Sekkei, one of Japan's largest architectural firms. The six-storey 1,428 square meter building contains a theatre and entertainment centre.

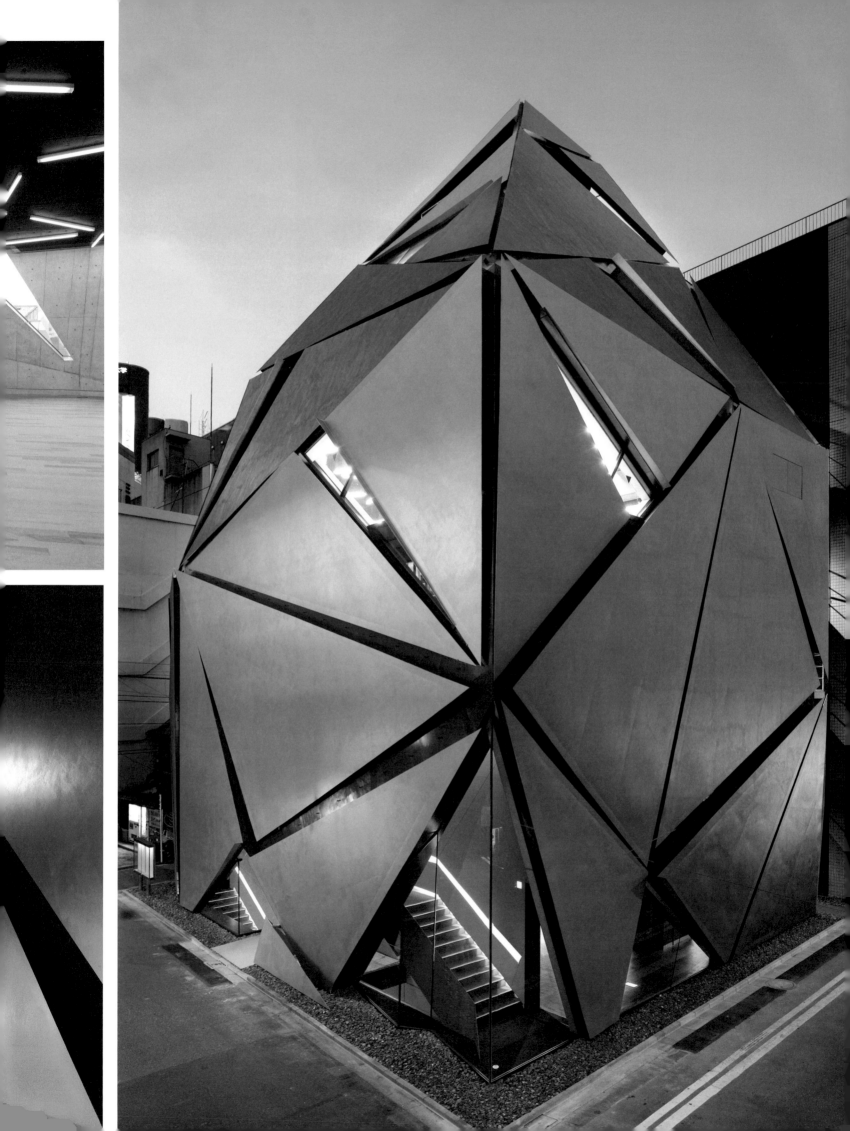

MANUELLE GAUTRAND ARCHITECTS
www.manuelle-gautrand.com

C42 Citroen Flagship Showroom
Paris, France, 2007

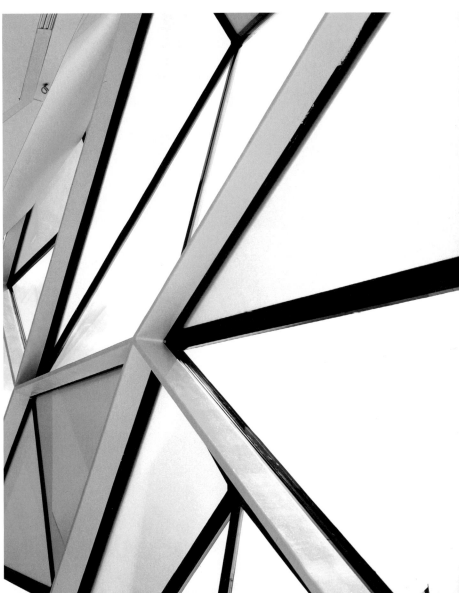

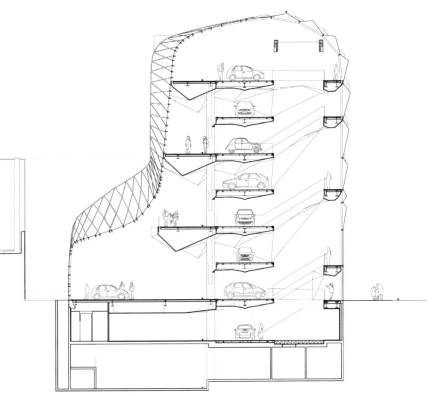

Longitudinal section

MAKE ARCHITECTS
www.makearchitects.com

55 Baker Street
London, United Kingdom, 2006

This radical renovation of a 1950s office building transforms the site into an important new urban amenity. While providing an exceptional range of flexible and highly efficient office spaces, the scheme enhances activity and interest at street level by offering an enriched mix of uses and introducing a substantial new public space to the streetscape.

Three glass infills or 'masks' span the voids between existing blocks to create a new facade for the building, with the central glazed section enclosing a seven-storey atrium which is open to the public. The ground floor of the building is entirely re-clad and devoted to retail units, cafes and restaurants serving residents, pedestrians and business employees. At the rear of the building, a new development of twenty-three houses offers affordable key worker and private accommodation.

Crazy Diamond

BIG / BJARKE INGELS GROUP
www.big.dk

VM Houses
Copenhagen, Denmark, 2005

The VM Houses complex, shaped like a V and an M when seen from above, is the first residential
project to be built in the new district of Copenhagen known as Ørestaden. The manipulated perimeter
block of the V building is clearly defined at its four corners, but open internally and along the sides.
Undue proximity to the neighbouring M house is eliminated by shifting the slab in its centre, ensur-
ing diagonal views to the vast, open fields around. As the first residential complex in the area, it was
important to the architects to create an inviting environment. To provide public space around the
buildings, the V volume is raised on five metre high columns, opening up the courtyard to the park
area on the south side, while the façades are articulated with niches and angles, creating a series of
informal meeting places.

Crazy Diamond

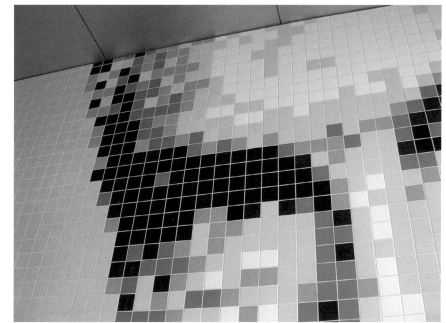

BARKOW LEIBINGER ARCHITECTS
www.barkowleibinger.com

TRUTEC Building
Seoul, Korea, 2007

The 11-storey mid-rise building by Berlin-based Barkow Leibinger Architects is clad in a skin of faceted reflective glass panels. The polygonal surfaces fragment any given contextual surroundings into a kaleidoscope of infinite pixels. The offset core of the building to the rear of the site allows large swathes of office spaces to access light at the street and side elevations. The ground floors are allocated to spacious showrooms for large machinery.

–288–

Crazy Diamond

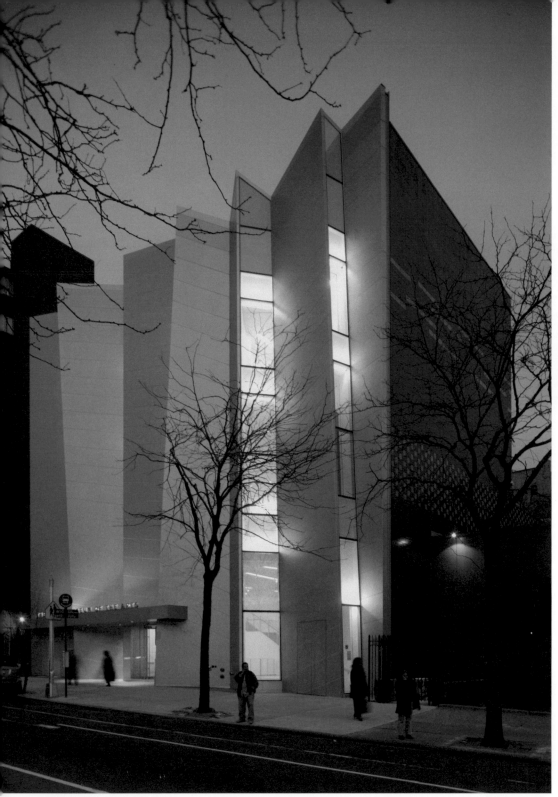

ARQUITECTONICA
www.arquitectonica.com

The Bronx Museum of the Arts
New York, USA, 2006

A new museum structure designed by Arquitectonica is mark-
ing the beginning of an ambitious plan to expand and eventually
replace the existing Bronx Art Museum. The first phase of the
project includes new galleries and administration spaces and an
outdoor sculpture court. Arquitectonica's first phase design grows
out of the sidewalk as an irregular folded screen made of fritted
glass and metallic panels. The resulting vertical zones of metal and
glass twist and turn like an architectural origami, demystifying the
wall on the street and making it permeable.

LYONS

www.lyonsarch.com.au

John Curtin School of Medical Research
Canberra, Australia, 2006

This new, low rise research and laboratory facility by Australian Lyons Architects is designed to enhance interactivity and collaborative research. The glazed entry foyer space incorporates interactive displays and a 200 seat public lecture theatre. The building incorporates landscaped courtyards, naturally ventilated offices and other ESD features.

Crazy Diamond

**FERNANDO MENIS
FELIPE ARTENGO RUFINO
J.M. RODRIGUEZ-PASTRANA**
www.menis.es; www.amparquitectos.com

MAGMA Art & Congress
Tenerife, Spain, 2005

MAGMA Arts and Congress appears as a reference point amongst anonymous buildings. The semi-desert landscape around it and the proximity of the sea, an imposing presence that frames the building establishing a strong relationship between both, and an impressive view over La Gomera island, are the starting points of the concept of the building. Thirteen geometrically shaped blocks emerge out from the base, housing all the functions such as offices, toilets, cafeteria, etc. and creating a light movement that generates the flow of the roof, outlining the space in every direction. In between these pieces there are the public spaces: hall, conference hall and congress hall, which accommodate different activities with a varying degree of division.

Crazy Diamond

-294-

Crazy Diamond

NEUTELINGS RIEDIJK ARCHITECTS
www.neutelings-riedijk.com

Central Tax Office
Apeldoorn, The Netherlands, 2007

The four existing and two new office towers of the Central Tax Office are bound together by a vast new plinth building. All communal functions such as congress centre, sports centre, restaurant, print shop, reception and parking are situated in this new extension. The plinth building is conceived as a dug out basement level around two large patio gardens. A huge rainwater pond covers the entire roof and is used as a cooling device for the building. A series of steel clad light wells float in the pond as the only visible elements of the sunken building.

Crazy Diamond

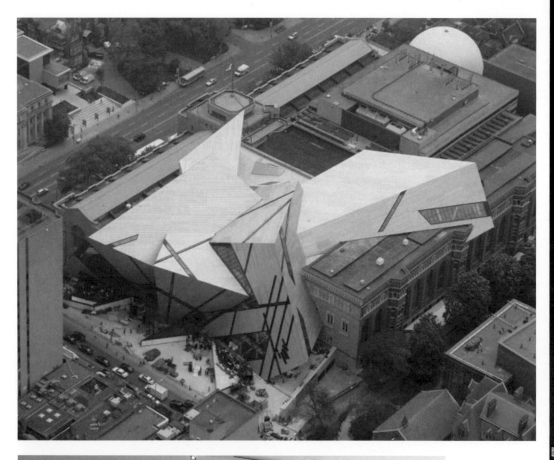

STUDIO DANIEL LIBESKIND
www.daniel-libeskind.com

Royal Ontario Museum
Toronto, Canada, 2007

The Royal Ontario Museum project set out to renovate ten new galleries in the existing historical building and to create an extension to the museum, now called the Michael Lee-Chin Crystal. This new extension provides innovative new architecture and creates a grand public attraction with a large new exhibition space. Situated at one of the most prominent intersections in downtown Toronto, the Museum has become a dynamic centre within the city.

Crazy Diamond

LAB ARCHITECTURE STUDIO
with Bates Smart
www.labarchitecture.com

Federation Square
Melbourne, Australia, 2002

Crazy Diamond

The Federation Square project created a new civic square for Melbourne, capable of accommodating up to 35,000 people in an open-air amphitheatre. The precinct comprises cultural and commercial buildings. These facilities cover almost 44,000 square meter and include new accommodation for the National Gallery of Victoria, various offices, studios and galleries and other facilities, as well as numerous restaurants, cafés and commercial tenancies. Federation Square creates a new urban order on a new site. More than just a new set of buildings, Federation Square is the new centre of cultural activity for Melbourne.

Crazy Diamond

Crazy Diamond

UN STUDIO
Ben van Berkel and Caroline Bos
www.unstudio.com

Agora Theatre
Lelystadt, Netherlands, 2006

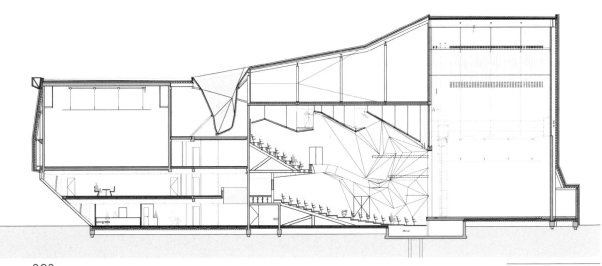

Crazy Diamond

Longitudinal section

Crazy Diamond

The Agora Theatre is an extremely colourful, determinedly upbeat place. The building is part of the masterplan for Lelystadt by Adriaan Geuze, which aims to revitalise the pragmatic, sober town centre. The theatre responds to the ongoing mission of reviving and recovering the post-war Dutch new towns by focusing on the arche-typal function of a theatre: that of creating a world of artifice and enchantment. Both inside and outside walls are faceted to reconstruct the kaleidoscopic experience of the world of the stage, where you can never be sure of what is real and what is not. In the Agora theatre drama and performance are not restricted to the stage and to the evening, but are extended to the urban experience and to daytime. Inside, the colourfulness of the outside increases in intensity; a handrail executed as a snak-ing pink ribbon cascades down the main staircase, winds itself all around the void at the centre of the large, open foyer space on the first floor and then extends up the wall towards the roof, optically changing colour all the while from violet, crimson and cherry to almost white.

STUDIO DANIEL LIBESKIND
www.daniel-libeskind.com

Contemporary Jewish Museum
San Francisco, USA, 2008

The design of the Contemporary Jewish Museum (CJM) in San Francisco provides a space for exhibitions, a place for activities and a symbol dedicated to the revitalisation of Jewish life in San Francisco and beyond. Inspired by the Hebrew phrase "I'chaim" (to life), the building is a physical embodiment of the museum's mission to bring together tradition and innovation in an exploration of the relevance of Jewish values and traditions in the 21st century.

Crazy Diamond

STUDIO DANIEL LIBESKIND

www.daniel-libeskind.com

Extension to the Denver Art Museum
Denver, USA, 2006

The extension to the Denver Art Museum, the Frederic C. Hamilton Building, is an expansion and addition to the existing museum, designed by the Italian Architect Gio Ponti. Inspired by the vitality and growth of Denver, the addition currently houses the modern and contemporary art collections as well as the collection of Oceanic and African art. The extension, which opened in October 2006, was a joint venture with Davis Partnership Architects, the Architect of Record, working with M.A. Mortensen Co. The new building is a kind of city hub, tying together the downtown Civic Center and forming a strong connection to the Golden Triangle neighbourhood. The project is not designed as a stand-alone building, but as part of the composition of public spaces, monuments and gateways in this developing part of the city. It contributes to synergy amongst its neighbours, both large and intimate.

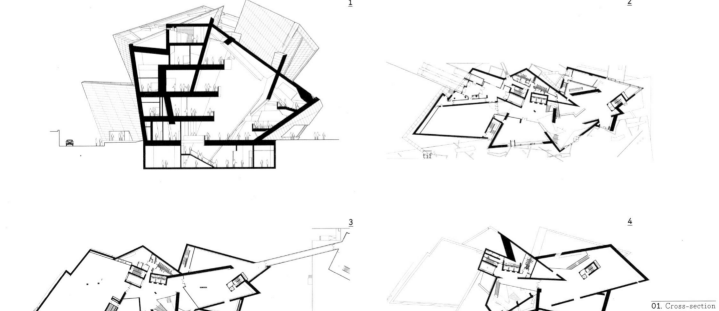

1

2

3

4

01. Cross-section
02. Ground floor plan
03. 2nd floor plan
04. 3rd floor plan

COOP HIMMELB(L)AU
Wolf D. Prix
www.coop-himmelblau.at

Akron Art Museum
Ohio, USA, 2007

Crazy Diamond

COOP HIMMELB(L)AU's Akron Art Museum should not be seen solely as an institution for the storage and display of knowledge: it is an urban concept, in which the zone between the city and the museum hybridises into a open space that engages the public in an urban discourse. The building is broken up into 3 parts: the Crystal, the Gallery Box, and the Roof Cloud. The Crystal serves as the main entrance and operates as an orientation and connection space serving both the new and the old building. The interior of the Gallery Box is an expansive space which has very few columns and is therefore extremely flexible for varying exhibition requirements. The Roof Cloud which hovers above the building creates a blurred envelope for the museum because of its sheer mass and materiality. It encloses interior spaces, provides shade for exterior spaces, and operates as a horizontal landmark in the city.

-313-

Crazy Diamond

NIKKEN SEKKEI
Makoto Wakabayashi and Hiroyuki Migitaka
www.nikken.co.jp

Modegakuen Spiral Towers
Nagoya, Japan, 2008

–314–

Crazy Diamond

INDEX.

INDEX.

INDEX.

INDEX.

[STRIKE A POSE].
ECCENTRIC <u>ARCHITECTURE</u> AND SPECTACULAR <u>SPACES</u>.

Edited by Robert Klanten and Lukas Feireiss
Text/Preface by Lukas Feireiss

Cover by Floyd Schulze for Gestalten
Layout by Floyd Schulze for Gestalten
Typefaces: Generell TW by Mika Mischler
Foundry: www.gestalten.com/fonts
Gravur Condensed by Cornel Windlin
Cover Photography by Tomaz Gregoric

Project management by Julian Sorge for Gestalten
Production management by Martin Bretschneider for Gestalten
Translation and copy editing by Michael Robinson
Proofreading by GlobalSprachTeam
Printed by Graphische Betriebe Eberl GmbH, Immenstadt i. Allgäu
Made in Germany

The title of the book and the titles of the four chapters were inspired by the following music songs:
"Vogue" (Madonna, Shep Pettibone) in: Madonna (1990): I'm Breathless - Music from and Inspired by the Film Dick Tracy, Sire / Warner Bros.
"Tramp" (Lowell Fulson, Jimmy McCracklin) in: Otis Redding and Carla Thomas (1967): King & Queen, Stax / Atlantic
"(I Want To Live On An) Abstract Plane" (Frank Black) in: Frank Black (1994): Teenager Of The Year, 4AD / Elektra
"True Colors" (Tom Kelly, Billy Steinberg) in: Cyndi Lauper (1986): True Colors, Portrait Records
"Shine On You Crazy Diamond" (David Gilmour, Roger Waters, Rick Wright) in: Pink Floyd (1975): Wish You Were Here, Harvest / Columbia

Published by Gestalten, Berlin 2008
ISBN 978-3-89955-225-6

For more information, please check www.gestalten.com

Bibliographic information published by the Deutsche Nationalbibliothek.
The Deutsche Nationalbibliothek lists this publication in the Deutsche Nationalbibliografie;
detailed bibliographic data is available on the internet at http://dnb.d-nb.de.

This book was printed according to the internationally accepted FSC standards for environmental
protection, which specify requirements for an environmental management system.

FSC **Mixed Sources**
Product group from well-managed
forests, controlled sources and
recycled wood or fiber
www.fsc.org Cert no. GFA-COC-001446
© 1996 Forest Stewardship Council

Gestalten is a climate neutral company and so are our products. We collaborate with the non-profit carbon offset
provider myclimate (www.myclimate.org) to neutralize the company's carbon footprint produced through our worldwide
business activities by investing in projects that reduce CO_2 emissions (www.gestalten.com/myclimate).

myclimate
Protect our planet